The Sassafras Guide to Chemistry

Written by Paige Hudson

> # THIS PRODUCT IS INTENDED FOR HOME USE ONLY
>
> The images and all other content in this book are copyrighted material owned by Elemental Science, Inc. Please do not reproduce this content on email lists or websites. If you have an eBook, you may print out as many copies as you need for use WITHIN YOUR IMMEDIATE FAMILY ONLY. Duplicating this book or printing the eBook so that the book can then be reused or resold is a violation of copyright.
>
> **Schools and co-ops:** You MAY NOT DUPLICATE OR PRINT any portion of this book for use in the classroom. Please contact us for licensing options at support@elementalscience.com.

The Sassafras Guide to Chemistry

First Edition 2023
Copyright @ Elemental Science, Inc.
Email: support@elementalscience.com

ISBN # 978-1-953490-19-3

Printed In USA For worldwide distribution

For more copies write to :
Elemental Science
PO Box 79
Niceville, FL 32588
support@elementalscience.com

Copyright Policy

All contents copyright ©2023 by Elemental Science. All rights reserved.

Limit of Liability and Disclaimer of Warranty: The publisher has used its best efforts in preparing this book, and the information provided herein is provided "as is." Elemental Science makes no representation or warranties with respect to the accuracy or completeness of the contents of this book and specifically disclaims any implied warranties of merchantability or fitness for any particular purpose and shall in no event be liable for any loss of profit or any other commercial damage, including but not limited to special, incidental, consequential, or other damages.

Trademarks: This book identifies product names and services known to be trademarks, registered trademarks, or service marks of their respective holders. They are used throughout this book in an editorial fashion only. In addition, terms suspected of being trademarks, registered trademarks, or service marks have been appropriately capitalized, although Elemental Science cannot attest to the accuracy of this information. Use of a term in this book should not be regarded as affecting the validity of any trademark, registered trademark, or service mark. Elemental Science is not associated with any product or vendor mentioned in this book.

Quick Start Guide

Welcome to your super, scientific journey with the Sassafras Twins!! The information and activities in this guide will help you turn a simple adventure novel into a complete science program for your elementary students. Let's start by answering three pressing questions!

What Will We Learn?

Students will learn about chemistry through a study of the periodic table. See p. 11 for a list of the topics explored in this program.

What Do I Need?

In addition to this activity guide, you will need the following materials:

1. **Novel** – *The Sassafras Science Adventures Volume 7: Chemistry* - All the main reading assignments are from this book. You can get the paperback novel, the Kindle version, or the audiobook.

2. **Student Materials** – You can have your students use a blank notebook or you can purchase a copy of *The Official Sassafras SCIDAT Logbook: Chemistry Edition* for each student. Get a glimpse of this option on p. 7. (SCIDAT stands for scientific data and it comes from the Sassafras Twins' journey.)

3. **Demonstration Supplies** – See p. 12 for a full list, or save yourself time and get the *Sassafras Science Year 4 Experiment Kit*, which includes the materials for both volume 7 and volume 8.

If you want more information than what is already in the novel, the following encyclopedias are scheduled in this guide:

- *DK Eyewitness: The Elements* (best for 2nd through 4th grades)
- *Scholastic's The Periodic Table* (best for 3rd through 5th grades)
- *Usborne Science Encyclopedia* (best for 3rd through 5th grades)
- *Kingfisher Science Encyclopedia* (best for 4th through 6th grades)

If you want to add more fun with optional STEAM* projects, you can find a list of the project supplies on p. 13.

*STEAM: Science, Technology, Engineering, Art, and Math

What Will a Week Look Like?

Each week you and your students will:

- **Read** scientific information from an adventure-filled novel, also known as a living book, and discuss what you read.

- **Write** down what the students have learned and seen in a way that is appropriate for their skills by keeping a notebook, or rather a SCIDAT Logbook.

- **Do** hands-on science through demonstrations using the directions found in this guide.

You can also add in the optional copywork, library books, and STEAM projects if you want to dig deeper into a topic. For a more detailed explanation of the components in each lesson, we highly recommend checking out the peek inside this guide on pp. 6-7 and reading the introduction on pp. 8-10. The chapter lessons begin on p. 17.

The Sassafras Guide to Chemistry
Table of Contents

Front Matter..3

    Quick Start Guide   3
    Activity Guide At-a-Glance   6
    The SCIDAT Logbook At-a-Glance   7
    Introduction   8
    Topical List   11
    Demonstration Supplies Listed By Chapter   12
    STEAM Project Supplies Listed By Chapter   13
    The Sassafras Guide to the Characters   14

Chapter Lessons..17

    Chapter 1: Schedules   18
    Chapter 1: Celebrating at the…   20

    Chapter 2: Schedules   24
    Chapter 2: 3 … 2 … 1 … Chemistry   26

    Chapter 3: Schedules   30
    Chapter 3: Launching Lunar Adventures   32

    Chapter 4: Schedules   36
    Chapter 4: Underground Siberian Science…   38

    Chapter 5: Schedules   42
    Chapter 5: Subterranean Dance-off   44

    Chapter 6: Schedules   48
    Chapter 6: Oh Iceland, Oh Iceland   50

    Chapter 7: Schedules   54
    Chapter 7: The Three Metals Quest   56

    Chapter 8: Schedules   60
    Chapter 8: The Masaki-Do Dojo   62

    Chapter 9: Schedules   66
    Chapter 9: The Nuclear Rescue Mission   68

    Chapter 10: Schedules   72
    Chapter 10: Singapore's Merlion Fashion…   74

    Chapter 11: Schedules   78
    Chapter 11: Models and Mysteries   80

    Chapter 12: Schedules   84
    Chapter 12: Britain's Carboxynitro Games   86

    Chapter 13: Schedules   90
    Chapter 13: The Three Challenges   92

Chapter 14: Schedules	96
Chapter 14: Iron Nails in Chilean Desert	98
Chapter 15: Schedules	102
Chapter 15: The Desert Dune Buggy Race	104
Chapter 16: Schedules	108
Chapter 16: On to Morocco	110
Chapter 17: Schedules	114
Chapter 17: Just a Bunch of Hot Air	116
Chapter 18: Schedules	120
Chapter 18: Zipping Back to Pecan Street	122

Appendix 125

Lab Report Sheet	127
Transition Metal Hunt	129
Periodic Table	130

Glossary 131

Book List 135

Quizzes 141

Chemistry Quiz #1	143
Chemistry Quiz #2	145
Chemistry Quiz #3	147
Chemistry Quiz #4	149
Chemistry Quiz #5	151
Chemistry Quiz #6	153
Chemistry Quiz #7	155
Chemistry Quiz #8	157

Activity Guide At-a-Glance

Take an adventure-filled journey to learn about science!

1. & 2. Scheduling Options

Choose from a grid-style schedule (1) or a list-style schedule (2). Either way, these scheduling options will make planning your weekly science adventure a snap! These schedule sheets include a summary of the chapter in case your students are reading the novel or listening to the audiobook on their own.

Read

3. Reading Assignments

Know what to read each week in the corresponding Sassafras Science novel. Plus, get options for additional encyclopedia pages to read and for books to check out from the library. The novel contains the essential information for each week, but if you want to dig deeper, we've got you covered!

Write

4. SCIDAT Logbook Info

Have confidence that your students are grasping the key points from the reading with the information in the notebooking section. Here, you will find the scientific details that were shared in the chapter, which could be included in your students' narrations or list of facts.

5. Relevant Vocabulary

Build your students' science vocabulary with words relevant to the topics the students are studying.

6. Copywork

Use these selections as memory work, copywork, or dictation—it's up to you!

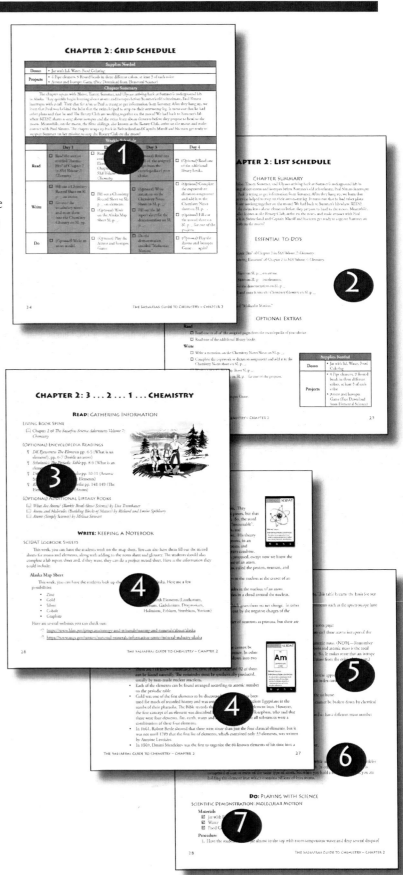

ACTIVITY GUIDE AT-A-GLANCE

DO

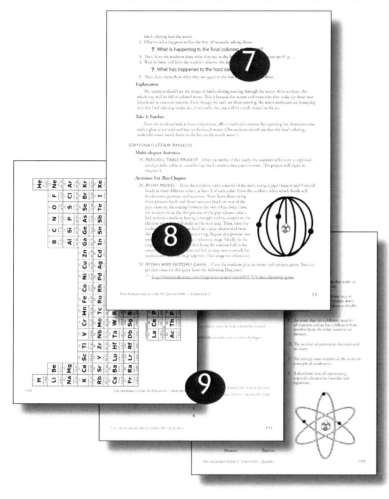

7. RELATED SCIENTIFIC DEMONSTRATIONS

Know what materials you will need to do a weekly hands-on science activity that coordinates with the topic. This section lists the supplies you will need, provides easy-to-follow steps, and explanations to make it a snap to complete the scientific demonstration.

8. COORDINATING STEAM* ACTIVITIES

Add in a bit of STEAM with these optional activity ideas. You will find ideas for projects that last throughout the novel and ones specific to the chapter (week) you are on.

9. TEMPLATES AND MORE

In the guide's appendix, you will find templates for the projects, a full glossary, and a set of quizzes to use along the journey.

*STEAM: Science, Technology, Engineering, Art, and Math

THE SCIDAT* LOGBOOK

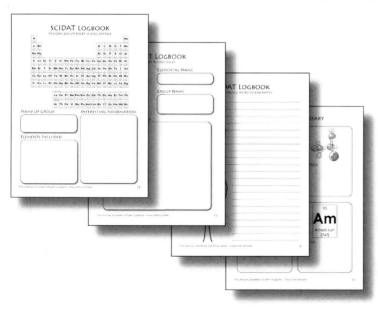

Don't forget the SCIDAT logbook for your students!!

The SCIDAT logbook will serve as a record of your students' journey! It contains all the pages the students will need as they follow like Blaine and Tracey. Each page has been attractively illustrated for you so you don't have to track down pictures for the students to use! Get it all at:

https://elementalscience.com/collections/ sassafras-science

*SCIDAT: Scientific Data

The Sassafras Guide to Chemistry
Introduction

Our living books method of science instruction was first proposed in *Success in Science: A Manual for Excellence in Science Education*. This approach is centered on living books that are augmented by notebooking and scientific demonstrations. The students read (or are read to) from a science-oriented living book, such as *The Sassafras Science Adventures Volume 7: Chemistry*. Then, they write about what they have learned and complete a related scientific demonstration or hands-on project. If time and interest allow, the teacher can add in non-fiction books that coordinate with the topic, do an additional activity, or memorize related information. If you want to learn more about how this works, you can listen to this free conference session on using living books for science:

Inspiring your students to love science through living books: https://youtu.be/Dvk1LfYGONw

The books in *The Sassafras Science Adventures* series are designed to give you the tools you need to employ the living books method of science instruction with your elementary students. For this reason, we have written an activity guide and a logbook that corresponds to each novel. This particular activity guide contains 18 chapters of activities, reading assignments, scientific demonstrations, and so much more for studying chemistry.

Each of the chapters in this guide corresponds directly to the chapters in *The Sassafras Science Adventures Volume 7: Chemistry*. They were written to give you the information you need to turn the adventure novel into a full science course for your elementary students. They will provide you with a buffet of options you can use to teach the students about the atoms, elements, and the periodic table. So pick and choose what you know you and your students will enjoy!

What Each Chapter Contains

Each chapter begins with two schedule sheets for the corresponding chapter in *The Sassafras Science Adventures Volume 7: Chemistry*. On the schedule sheets, you will find a chapter summary, plus an overview of the supplies you will need for the demonstration, projects, and activities for the chapter. After that, you will find the optional schedules – one laid out as a four-day grid schedule and one laid out as a list to check off. These schedules are included to give you an idea of how your week could be organized, so please feel free to alter them to suit your needs.

After the scheduling information, you will find the information for the reading, notebooking, and activities for the particular chapter. This information is divided into the following sections:

Read: Gathering Information

- Living Book Spine – This section contains the corresponding chapter in *The Sassafras Science Adventures Volume 7: Chemistry*.

- (Optional) Encyclopedia Readings – This section contains possible reading assignments from:
  - *DK Eyewitness: The Elements* (best for 2nd through 4th grades)
  - *Scholastic's The Periodic Table* (best for 3rd through 5th grade)
  - *Usborne Science Encyclopedia* (best for 3rd through 5th grade)

- *Kingfisher Science Encyclopedia* (best for 4th through 6th grades)

  You can choose to read them to the students or have the students read them on their own.

- 📖 **(Optional) Additional Library Books** – This section contains a list of books that coordinate with what is being studied in the chapter. You can check these books out of your local library.

Write: Keeping a Notebook

- 📓 **SCIDAT Logbook Information** – This section has the information that the students could have included in their SCIDAT logbooks. (SCIDAT stands for scientific data and it comes from the Sassafras Twins' journey.) The students may or may not have the same information on their notebooking sheets, which is fine. You want their SCIDAT logbooks to be a record of what they have learned. The logbook information is included as a guide for you to use as you check their work. For more information about notebooking, please read the following article:
  - 🖱 What is notebooking? – https://elementalscience.com/blogs/news/what-is-notebooking
  - 🖱 How to use notebooking with different ages – https://elementalscience.com/blogs/news/notebooking-with-different-ages

- ✏ **Vocabulary** – This section includes vocabulary words that coordinate with each chapter. If the students are older, we recommend that you have them create a glossary of terms using a blank sheet of lined paper or the glossary sheets provided in *The Official Sassafras Student SCIDAT Logbook: Chemistry Edition*. You can also have them memorize these words and their definitions.

- ☞ **(Optional) Copywork** – This section contains a short copywork passage and a longer dictation passage for you to use. Some students may use the shorter passages for dictation or the longer passages for copywork. Feel free to tailor the selections to your students' abilities. You can also use the selections as memory work assignments for the students.

- ⌛ **(Optional) Quiz** – This section contains the answers for the quizzes included in the appendix. These simple, short quizzes are optional. You can use them as graded quizzes or as review sheets.

Do: Playing with Science

- ☑ **Scientific Demonstration** – This section includes a list of materials, the instructions, and an explanation for a scientific demonstration that coordinates with the chapter. There is a customized lab report sheet provided for you in *The Official Sassafras Student SCIDAT Logbook: Chemistry Edition* or you can use the blank one in the appendix on pp. 127-128. If you student has followed the twins' journey so far, they are mostly likely at the age where they should be officially recording all of the demonstrations they do. If this is too much for your student, feel free to skip the lab reports.

- ✂ **(Optional) STEAM* Projects** – These sections contain additional STEAM projects and activities that correspond to the topics in the chapter. There are multi-chapter activities that students can do over the course of several chapters or over the full novel. Plus, there are activities that coordinate with each specific chapter. Pick and choose the activities that interest you and your students.

*STEAM: Science, Technology, Engineering, Art, and Math

Additional Materials

We have provided a few additional materials in the back of this guide for your convenience. First, you will find the templates you need for the projects suggested in this guide. Next, you will find a glossary of terms, which you can use with the students as they define the words for each chapter. And finally, you will find a set of eight simple quizzes you can use with the students to verify they are retaining the material.

Quick Links

View all the links mentioned in this guide in one place and get a digital copy of the templates, glossary, and quizzes by visiting the following page:

https://elementalscience.com/blogs/resources/volume-7-links

For the students

The SCIDAT logbook is meant to be a record of the students' journey through their study of chemistry. It is explained in more detail in Chapter 1 of this guide. You can choose to make your own or purchase a premade logbook from Elemental Science. *The Official Sassafras SCIDAT Logbook: Chemistry Edition* has all the pages the students will need to create their own logbook. Each page has been attractively illustrated for you so you don't have to track down pictures for the students to use. This way they can focus on the information they are learning.

Final Thoughts

As the author and publisher of this curriculum I encourage you to contact me with any questions or problems that you might have concerning *The Sassafras Guide to Chemistry* at support@elementalscience.com. I, or a member of our team, will be more than happy to assist you. I hope that you and your students enjoy your journey through the periodic table with the Sassafras twins!

~ Paige Hudson

TOPICAL LIST

The Sassafras Science Adventures Volume 7: Chemistry covers a variety of aspects of chemistry, such as:

- Compounds
- Reactions
- Atoms
- Isotopes
- Elements
- The Periodic Table
- Acids and Bases
- Mixtures and Solutions
- States of Matter
- Oxidation and Reduction
- Magnetism
- Nuclear Energy
- Conductivity
- Organic Chemistry
- Minerals
- Bonding
- Electrolysis
- Distillation
- Air
- Hydrocarbons
- Polymers

In the process, you will learn about the following specific elements and groups:

- Hydrogen
- Alkali Metals
- Sodium
- Potassium
- Alkaline Earth Metals
- Magnesium
- Calcium
- Transition Metals
- Gold
- Zinc
- Iron
- Lanthanides
- Neodymium
- Actinides
- Uranium
- Main Group Metals
- Aluminum
- Metalloids
- Silicon
- Nonmetals
- Carbon
- Oxygen
- Nitrogen
- Halogens
- Chlorine
- Iodine
- Noble Gases
- Helium
- Neon

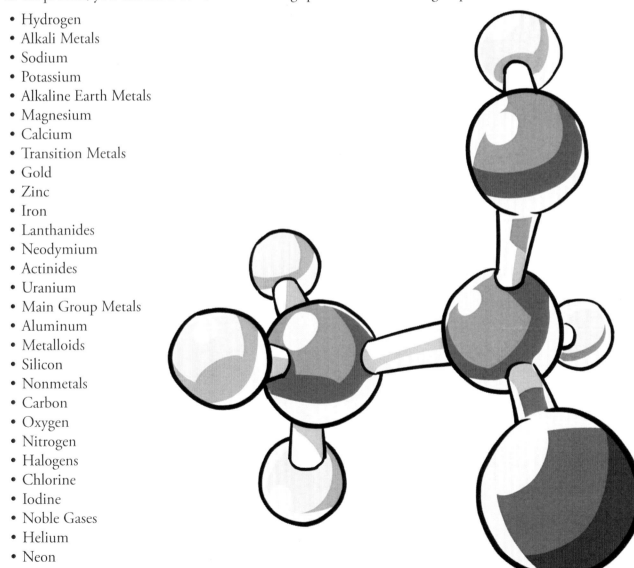

Demonstration Supplies Listed By Chapter

Chapter	Supplies Needed
1: Chemical Reaction	Clear glass cup or bowl, White vinegar, Milk
2: Molecular Motion	Jar with lid, Water, Food Coloring
3: Table Sorting	LEGO® bricks - a variety of colors and sizes (you can also used stuffed animals, buttons, beads, or any other object with different sizes and colors if you don't have any LEGO bricks), Paper, Pen
4: Which one freezes first?	3 Cups, Water, Food coloring, Salt
5: Magnesium Solutions	Epsom salts, Ammonia, Water, Clear cup
6: Metal Plating	White vinegar, Salt, 6 Pennies, Glass cup, 2 Iron nails
7: Rusted	Steel wool, Vinegar, Jar with lid
8: Magnetic Exploration	Neodymium magnets, Several types of objects (marbles, paper clips, paper, pins, plastic spoons, and more)
9: Radioactive Decay	Bite-sized food, such as raisins or cereal puffs or M&M's, Timer
10: Aluminum Gel	Alum powder, Ammonia, Clear jar, Water
11: Silicone Putty	Silly Putty™ or other silicone polymer, Baggie, Ice, Bowl, Hot water
12: Shiny Pennies	Can of dark cola soda, Glass, Dirty pennies
13: Oxygen Overflow	Yeast, Water, Cup, Empty water bottle, Hydrogen peroxide, Food coloring, Liquid dish soap
14: Fluoride Help	2 Eggs, Toothpaste with fluoride, Plastic wrap, White vinegar, 2 Cups, Permanent marker
15: Iodine Swab	Small piece of potato or a piece of bread, Iodine swab
16: Funny Voice	Helium-filled balloon, Scissors
17: Air In There	Small cup, Tissue paper, Water, Bucket or large bowl
18: Periodic Table Match-up	Periodic Table Match-up Cards (free download from Elemental Science)

STEAM Project Supplies Listed By Chapter

The multi-chapter and specific chapter STEAM projects listed in this guide are optional, so you may not need all of these supplies. However, this list has been provided for your convenience. If you do decide to do these projects, in addition to the items listed each week you will need glue, scissors, a variety of paint colors, and a set of markers.

Chapter	Supplies Needed
1	LEGO® bricks
2	4 Pipe cleaners, 9 Round beads in three different colors, at least 3 of each color, Atoms and Isotopes Game (free download from Elemental Science)
3	Red cabbage, Water, Pot, A variety of liquids or powders from your kitchen (such as lemon juice, baking soda, soda, or detergent), and Several cups
4	Cup, Baking Soda, Vinegar, Coffee filter, Rubbing alcohol, Eyedropper, Jar, Rubber band, Permanent markers in a variety of colors, Heavy cream, Milk, Sugar, Vanilla, 1 quart-sized Ziploc plastic baggie, Crushed ice, 1 gallon-sized Ziploc plastic baggie, Rock salt
5	Egg, White vinegar, Clear Glass, Pot, Water, Green veggie of your choice, Baking soda
6	3 Balloons, Water, Ice
7	A tarnished silver item (jewelry or silverware), Tongs, Bowl, Aluminum foil, Baking soda, Hot water, Breakfast cereal, Strong magnet, Paper
8	Woolen mitten or glove. Fluorescent bulb, White glue, Water, Iron filings, Borax, Small neodymium magnets
9	A working smoke detector, Bottle of baby powder, Computer with Internet access
10	*No additional supplies needed*
11	Gel glue, Water, Borax powder, Magic sand
12	Limestone or chalk, Cup, White vinegar
13	Candle, Match, Glass jar
14	2 Colors of paint, Paper, A few pom-pom balls, Pencil eraser
15	Iodine, Water, Cup, Vitamin C, Shallow pan, Tincture of iodine, Water, Paper, Q-tip, Lemon juice, Cup
16	*No additional supplies needed*
17	Balloon
18	Vegetable oil, Cornstarch, Water, Food coloring, Plastic bag, Eyedropper, White (or clear gel) glue, Water, Plastic baggie, Borax

The Sassafras Guide to the Characters Found in Volume 7: Chemistry

Cecil's Neighborhood (Chapter 1)

★ **Tracey Sassafras**§ – She is the female twin of the almost famous duo known as the Sassafras twins. She is an avid ambidextrous bowler and riddle solver. She is also known as Blaisey, Fish Hook, and Tracey the Plucky.

★ **Blaine Sassafras**§ – He is the male twin of the almost famous duo known as the Sassafras twins. He is an aspiring break-dancer in his own mind, and his ambidextrous bowling record is average. He is also known as Train, Rowboat, and Blaine the Handsome.

★ **Cecil Sassafras**§ – He is the one and only uncle to the Sassafras twins who will probably never get their names right. He is also the ambidextrous bowler responsible for the legendary octo-bowl. He is the inventor and scientist responsible for the twins' summer of science.

★ **Summer Beach**§ – She is a most unique, sandwich-loving scientist! She has brought her infectious energy to every leg of the twins' journey so far. She's Cecil's schoolmate turned best friend and a *pro re nata* agent for the Triple S (Swiss Secret Service).

★ **President Lincoln**§ – This legendary prairie dog serves as Uncle Cecil's right-hand paw. He is a reticent animal with a brilliant mind and is known as the second-best ambidextrous animal bowler. He is also known as The Prez and Linc Dog.

★ **Ulysses S. Grant**§ – This mythical Arctic ground squirrel lends a paw to all that Summer does in her underground lab. He is a snappy inventor and holds the title of "Number 1 Ambidextrous Animal Bowler."

★ **Yang Bo**§ * – He is the astronaut who served as the twins' local expert on the International Space Station. He is also a former classmate of Uncle Cecil and Summer from middle school.

★ **Wiggles and Fidget**§ – They are the museum security guards the twins first met on their astronomy leg.

★ **Captain Marolf**§ – He is the head of the Triple S. He also appeared in the twins' Earth science and astronomy legs.

Alaska and the Moon (Chapters 2-3)

★ **Paul Sims**§ – He is the museum curator at the National Air and Space Museum. He is also a friend and schoolmate of Cecil's and Summer's who is hiding quite a bit.

★ **The Rotary Club** – This club is made up of the Slote siblings: Alexander, Graham, and Belle. They are against technology and will do almost anything to return the world to rotary phone usage.

★ **REESE** – This joint invention of President Lincoln and Ulysses S. Grant is a robot whose name stands for Robotic Exploration, Entertainment, and Scientific Enhancement.

★ **Jorgen Wuthrich** – He is the Triple S agent and partner to Agent DeBlose's whom the twins met on their Earth science leg.

★ **Evan DeBlose*** – A lead Triple S Agent and earth science local expert. He was quite busy on the twins' astronomy leg taking down the rogue Agent Adrianne Archer and the nefarious Yuroslav Bogdanovich.

★ **Mr. Womberfraggle**§ * – He was Uncle Cecil's and Summer's middle school chemistry teacher.

§ These characters appear throughout the novel. We have chosen to share about them in the chapter where they first appear.

* These characters are only mentioned in the text but are not a part of this leg of the journey.

Siberia (Chapters 4-5)

★ **Rodi Abramov** – He acts as the twins' local expert for their time in Siberia. He and his sister, Dina, were hired by the Turgenev Mining Company to bring science and joviality to the mining operation.
★ **Dina Abramov** – She is Rodi's sister and sidekick in science and joviality.
★ **Trof** – He is one of the miners who worked in the Siberian mine. He doesn't like science . . . or joviality.
★ **Taras** – He is another of the miners who worked in the Siberian mine. He starts to see how amazing knowing about science can be!
★ **The Man With No Eyebrows**[§] – He is the memory-erasing, disappearing cape-wearing, eyebrow-less man who has tried just about everything he can think of to stop the twins. His real name is Thaddeus, and it turns out that he was a schoolmate of Cecil's and Summer's.
★ **Sveta Corvette** – She is the neon-green punk-rocker who once traveled the trains as a stowaway, but now she is a star of the band Sveta and the Spark Plugs.

Iceland (Chapters 6-7)

★ **Ingrid the Hospitable** – She is the beautiful female member of the Kunningskapur, which is a guild of adventurers in Iceland who seek the three metals.
★ **Harland the Wise** – He is the blonde-headed male member of the Kunningskapur and the twins' local expert of their Iceland leg.
★ **Magnus the Brave** – He is the red-headed, short-tempered male member of the Kunningskapur.
★ **Dagfinn the Wicked** – He is the brawny, dark-haired opponent of the Kunningskapur.

Japan (Chapters 8-9)

★ **Sensei Masaki** – He is the twins' local expert for their leg in Japan and the head of the Masaki-do Dojo.
★ **Haipa Yagi (or Hyper Goat)** – He is a member of the Masaki-do Dojo in Japan. His given name is Seth E. Prue, and he is the only non-Japanese student at the dojo.
★ **Hageshi Tora (or Fierce Tiger)** – She is a member of the Masaki-do Dojo in Japan. She's not afraid of anything.
★ **Chiteki Kirin (or Intelligent Giraffe)** – She is a member of the Masaki-do Dojo in Japan. Her proverbial mind can outsmart anyone.
★ **Attosuru Tonbo (or Overpowering Dragonfly)** – He is a member of the Masaki-do Dojo in Japan. He is short but incredibly determined.
★ **Sairento Sai (Silent Rhino)** – He is a member of the Masaki-do Dojo in Japan. He doesn't speak, but he is one of the strongest ninjas in the entire dojo.
★ **Hayato Doi** – He is a rich, power-hungry businessman who has an army of evil ninjas known as the Jaken.
★ **Natsuki Saito** – She is the CEO of the A.B.G. Nuclear Power Plant.

Singapore (Chapters 10-11)

★ **Aishaanya** – She is a fashion icon and designer

in the Singapore fashion scene who owns Aishaanya Inc. She is the twins' local expert for their time in Singapore.
- **Brutus** – He is Aishaanya's bodyguard.
- **Tamina** – She is a former employee of Aishaanya. She left under not-so-great circumstances and went on to start her own fashion business.
- **Sadie Nichols** – She is a news anchor for THE DROP.
- **Grady** – He is Sadie's cameraman.
- **Bisaam** – He is one of the technology experts and conceptual artists at Aishaanya Inc.
- **Rosemary Rajan** – She is one of Aishaanya's new and upcoming designers.

Great Britain (Chapters 12-13)

- **The Unseen One** – He fulfills the role of the twins' local expert for their time in Great Britain. His voice is heard throughout the Carboxynitro Games but he's not necessarily seen.
- **The Davies twins** – They are a blonde-headed set of twin boys participating in the Carboxynitro Games.
- **The Edward twins** – They are a red-headed set of twin girls participating in the Carboxynitro Games.
- **The Clark twins** – They are a set of boy-girl twins participating in the Carboxynitro Games.
- **Tom** – He is a former colleague of the Unseen One.

Chile (Chapters 14-15)

- **Rose Rock** – She serves as the twins' local expert in Chile. She is a chemist, a teacher, the daughter of the chief, and a strong supporter of the villagers.
- **Ring Finger** – He is the War Lord King of the Atacama Desert.
- **The Iron Nails** – They are a band of men who enforce the will of Ring Finger.
- **Vicente** – He is Rose's good friend who also happens to be deaf.
- **Maximiliano** – Another villager who is intent on beating Rose Rock.

Morocco (Chapters 16-17)

- **The SAM Collective** – They are a group of three scientists, activists, and mathematicians—Samir, Sami, and Samirah—who provide the local expert information for the twins in Morocco.
- **The A.S.M. (Anonymous Snake charmers of Morocco)** – They are a gang of hundreds of ruffians who charm snakes in Morocco.

Chapter Lessons

Chapter 1: Grid Schedule

Supplies Needed	
Demo	• Clear glass cup or bowl, White vinegar, Milk
Projects	• LEGO® bricks

Chapter Summary

The chapter opens with Tracey, Blaine, Uncle Cecil, Summer, President Lincoln, and Ulysses S. Grant bowling at the Ambidextrous Octopus. It was girls against boys, plus lab assistants—of course the girls won! After the game wrapped up, the review presentation for the twins' astronomy leg began. Afterward, Uncle Cecil ended up making a legendary octo-bowl that even Ollie the Octopus, the bowling alley's mascot, couldn't believe. Among the congratulations that ensued, there was an awkward moment between Cecil and Summer that made the twins wonder what was going on. This was quickly interrupted by a phone call from Captain Marolf—the Swiss Secret Service needed Summer's help in space and the twins were going to join her. As the chapter ends, it is time to head out on the seventh leg of the journey to learn about chemistry!

Weekly Schedule

	Day 1	**Day 2**	**Day 3**	**Day 4**
Read	☐ Read the section entitled "Astronomical Bowling" of Chapter 1 in *SSA* Volume 7: Chemistry*.	☐ (*Optional*) Read one or all of the assigned pages from the encyclopedia of your choice.	☐ Read the section entitled "Chemical Departure" of Chapter 1 in *SSA Volume 7: Chemistry*.	☐ (*Optional*) Read one of the additional library books.
Write	☐ Set up your students' SCIDAT logbooks.	☐ (*Optional*) Write a narration on the Chemistry Notes Sheet on SL** p. 7. ☐ Fill out the lab report sheet for the demonstration on SL p. 6.	☐ Go over the vocabulary words and enter them into the Chemistry Glossary on SL p. 102.	☐ (*Optional*) Complete the copywork or dictation assignment and add it to the Chemistry Notes Sheet on SL p. 7.
Do	☐ (*Optional*) Play "I Spy."	☐ Do the demonstration entitled "Chemical Reaction."	☐ (*Optional*) Make Molecule Models.	

*SSA = *The Sassafras Science Adventures*
**SL = *The Official Sassafras SCIDAT Logbook: Chemistry Edition*

Chapter 1: List Schedule

Chapter Summary

The chapter opens with Tracey, Blaine, Uncle Cecil, Summer, President Lincoln, and Ulysses S. Grant bowling at the Ambidextrous Octopus. It was girls against boys, plus lab assistants—of course the girls won! After the game wrapped up, the review presentation for the twins' astronomy leg began. Afterward, Uncle Cecil ended up making a legendary octo-bowl that even Ollie the Octopus, the bowling alley's mascot, couldn't believe. Among the congratulations that ensued, there was an awkward moment between Cecil and Summer that made the twins wonder what was going on. This was quickly interrupted by a phone call from Captain Marolf—the Swiss Secret Service needed Summer's help in space and the twins were going to join her. As the chapter ends, it is time to head out on the seventh leg of the journey to learn about chemistry!

Essential To-Do's

Read
- ☐ Read the section entitled "Astronomical Bowling" of Chapter 1 in *SSA* Volume 7: Chemistry*.
- ☐ Read the section entitled "Chemical Departure" of Chapter 1 in *SSA Volume 7: Chemistry*.

Write
- ☐ Set up your students' SCIDAT logbooks.
- ☐ Fill out the lab report sheet for the demonstration on SL** p. 6.
- ☐ Go over the vocabulary words and enter them into the Chemistry Glossary on SL p. 102.

Do
- ☐ Do the demonstration entitled "Chemical Reaction."

Optional Extras

Read
- ☐ Read one or all of the assigned pages from the encyclopedia of your choice.
- ☐ Read one of the additional library books.

Write
- ☐ Write a narration on the Chemistry Notes Sheet on SL p. 7.
- ☐ Complete the copywork or dictation assignment and add it to the Chemistry Notes Sheet on SL p. 7.

Do
- ☐ Play "I Spy."
- ☐ Make Molecule Models.

*SSA = *The Sassafras Science Adventures*
**SL = *The Official Sassafras SCIDAT Logbook: Chemistry Edition*

Supplies Needed	
Demo	• Clear glass cup or bowl, White vinegar, Milk
Projects	• LEGO® bricks

Chapter 1: Celebrating at the Ambidextrous Octopus

READ: Gathering Information

Living Book Spine

📖 Chapter 1 of *The Sassafras Science Adventures Volume 7: Chemistry*

(Optional) Encyclopedia Readings

- *DK Eyewitness: The Elements* (no pages scheduled)
- *Scholastic's The Periodic Table* (no pages scheduled)
- *Usborne Science Encyclopedia* pp. 14-15 (Molecules), pp. 76-77 (Chemical Reactions)
- *Kingfisher Science Encyclopedia* pp. 162-163 (Chemical Reactions), pp. 164-165 (Chemical Compounds)

(Optional) Additional Library Books

📖 *Atoms and Molecules (Why Chemistry Matters)* by Molly Aloian
📖 *Atoms and Molecules (My Science Library)* by Tracy Nelson Maurer

WRITE: Keeping a Notebook

SCIDAT Logbook Sheets

This chapter, you will set up the students' SCIDAT logbooks. You can use blank sheets of copy paper with dividers for each section or purchase *The Official Sassafras Student SCIDAT Logbook: Chemistry Edition* with all the pages and pictures from Elemental Science. For each of these sheets, you can have the students enter information only from *The Sassafras Science Adventures Volume 7: Chemistry*, or you can have them do additional research to gather more facts. The following video shares a peek inside a 2nd-grader's SCIDAT Logbook:

🖱 https://www.youtube.com/watch?v=0m4nj-K7s58

What you choose to do will depend upon the ages and abilities of your students. Below is an explanation of each of the student sheets.

Chemistry Record Sheets

The purpose of these sheets is for the students to record what they have learned about the topics that are introduced in *The Sassafras Science Adventures Volume 7: Chemistry*.

INFORMATION LEARNED: The students should color the picture above the box, if they desire, and enter any information that they have learned about the particular topic.

Element Record Sheets

The purpose of these sheets is for the students to record what they have learned about the elements that are covered in *The Sassafras Science Adventures Volume 7: Chemistry*.

> **ELEMENTAL NAME:** Have the students write down the name of the element that was studied.
>
> **GROUP NAME:** Have the students add the name of the group that the element is a part of.
>
> **INFORMATION LEARNED:** Have the students enter any information that they have learned about the particular element.

Periodic Group Sheets

The purpose of these sheets is to give the students an opportunity to record what they have learned about the groups in the periodic table.

> **PERIODIC TABLE IMAGE:** Have the students color the elements included in the group on the periodic table image.
>
> **GROUP NAME:** Have the students add the name of the group of elements.
>
> **ELEMENTS INCLUDED:** Have the students name the elements included in the group.
>
> **INTERESTING INFORMATION:** Have the students enter anything they have found interesting about the group of elements.

Customized Lab Report Sheets

The purpose of these sheets is for the students to record the demonstrations they have done during the course of their study of chemistry.

Map Sheets

The purpose of these sheets are to give your students an opportunity to do a bit of research because the answers for these will not all be covered in the novel. Instead, the students will need to look them up on the Internet or in an atlas that shows a region's industry and resources, such as *DK Children's Illustrated Atlas*.

> **WORLD MAP IMAGE:** Have the students color the region where the twins have traveled.
>
> **MINERALS:** Have the students look up and write down any minerals found in the region, for example, gold, bauxite, and so on.
>
> **INDUSTRY:** Have the students look up and write down any industry that involves chemistry, for example, oil, gas, nuclear power, and so on.

Chemistry Notes Sheets

The purpose of these sheets is for the students to record any additional information that they have learned during their study of chemistry. You can use these sheets to record additional narrations, copywork, or dictation assignments.

Project Record Sheets

The purpose of these sheets is for the students to record the projects they have done during the course of their study of chemistry.

Chemistry Glossary

The purpose of the glossary is for the students to create a dictionary of terms that they have encountered while reading *The Sassafras Science Adventures Volume 7: Chemistry*. They can look up each term in a science encyclopedia or in the glossary included on pp. 133-134 of this guide. Then have the students copy each definition onto a blank index card or into their SCIDAT logbooks. They should also illustrate each of the vocabulary words. (NOTE—In *The Official Sassafras Student SCIDAT Logbook: Chemistry Edition*, these pictures are already provided.)

Vocabulary

Have the older students look up the following terms in the glossary in the appendix on pp. 133-134 or in a science encyclopedia. Then, have them copy the definition onto a blank index card or into their SCIDAT logbook.

- CHEMICAL REACTION – An occurrence where the atoms in substances are rearranged to form new substances.
- MOLECULE – A substance made up of two or more atoms that are chemically bonded.

(Optional) Copywork

Copywork Selection

Most of the elements are not found in their purest form. Instead, they are found in compounds.

Dictation Passage

Compounds are substances that are composed of two or more elements. There are two types of compounds found on Earth: organic compounds and inorganic compounds. Organic compounds are those that support life and contain carbon. Inorganic compounds are salts, metals, and other elemental compounds.

Do: Playing with Science

Scientific Demonstration: Chemical Reaction

Materials
- ☑ Clear glass cup or bowl
- ☑ White vinegar (apple cider vinegar will work too, but not as well)
- ☑ Milk

Procedure
1. Add ¼ cup of vinegar to a clear glass or bowl.
2. Then, add ¾ cup of milk, and stir gently to mix.
3. Wait fifteen minutes, and observe the changes that have occurred, asking the students the following:

    ? What happened to the milk in the cup?

4. Have the students fill out a report sheet for this demonstration.

Explanation

The students should see that the milk changes from a smooth liquid to a chunky mess. This is because the acid in the vinegar causes the proteins to in the milk to bind together, producing a chemical change. This change is a chemical reaction.

Take It Further

Have the students do another simple chemical reaction involving baking soda and vinegar. Have them add a few tablespoons of vinegar to the bottom of a glass. Then, have them sprinkle about a teaspoon of baking soda into the glass and watch what happens. (NOTE—You will want to do this in the sink or in a tub because it has a tendency to spill over.)

(Optional) STEAM Projects

Multi-chapter Activities

- **Periodic Table Project** – Over the weeks of this study, the students will create a large, wall-sized periodic table or a small, lap-sized construction-paper version. This project will begin in Chapter 3.

Activities For This Chapter

- **I Spy** – Play a game of "I Spy" to help the students work on their observation skills.

- **Molecule Models** – Have the students make molecules models out of LEGO® bricks using the examples from the following pin:

    https://www.pinterest.com/pin/192036371586132562/

    NOTE—Are they molecules or compounds? Molecules are formed when two or more atoms join together. Compounds are formed when two or more elements join together. For example H_2 (hydrogen gas) is a molecule because two atoms of hydrogen are joined together. However, because there is only one type of element present, H_2 is not a compound. In contrast, H_2O (water) is a molecule because the three atoms, one oxygen atom and two hydrogen atoms, have been joined together to form it. It is also a compound because it contains two different elements, hydrogen

Chapter 2: Grid Schedule

Supplies Needed	
Demo	• Jar with lid, Water, Food Coloring
Projects	• 4 Pipe cleaners, 9 Round beads in three different colors, at least 3 of each color • Atoms and Isotopes Game (free download from Elemental Science)

Chapter Summary

The chapter opens with Blaine, Tracey, Summer, and Ulysses arriving back at Summer's underground lab in Alaska. They quickly begin learning about atoms and isotopes before Summer's old schoolmate, Paul Simms, interrupts with a call. They chat for a bit because Paul is trying to get information from Summer. After they hang up, we learn that Paul was behind the heist that the twins helped stop on their astronomy leg. It turns out that he had other plans and that he and the Rotary Club are working together on the moon! We head back to Summer's lab, where REESE shares a song about isotopes and the twins learn about elements before they prepare to head to the moon. Meanwhile, the Slote siblings, also known as the Rotary Club, arrive on the moon and make contact with Paul Simms. The chapter wraps up back in Switzerland, and Captain Marolf and his team get ready to support Summer on her mission to stop the Rotary Club on the moon!

Weekly Schedule

	Day 1	Day 2	Day 3	Day 4
Read	☐ Read the section entitled "Atomic Bits" of Chapter 2 in *SSA Volume 7: Chemistry*.	☐ Read the section entitled "Dancing Elements" of Chapter 2 in *SSA Volume 7: Chemistry*.	☐ (*Optional*) Read one or all of the assigned pages from the encyclopedia of your choice.	☐ (*Optional*) Read one of the additional library books.
Write	☐ Fill out a Chemistry Record Sheet on SL p. 9 on atoms. ☐ Go over the vocabulary words and enter them into the Chemistry Glossary on SL pp. 102-103.	☐ Fill out a Chemistry Record Sheet on SL p. 10 on elements. ☐ (*Optional*) Work on the Alaska Map Sheet on SL p. 17.	☐ (*Optional*) Write narration on the Chemistry Notes Sheet on SL p. 15. ☐ Fill out the lab report sheet for the demonstration on SL p. 13.	☐ (*Optional*) Complete the copywork or dictation assignment and add it to the Chemistry Notes Sheet on SL p. 15. ☐ (*Optional*) Fill out the record sheet on SL p. 18 for one of the projects.
Do	☐ (*Optional*) Make an Atom Model.	☐ (*Optional*) Play the Atoms and Isotopes Game.	☐ Do the demonstration entitled "Molecular Motion."	☐ (*Optional*) Play the Atoms and Isotopes Game . . . again!

Chapter 2: List Schedule

Chapter Summary

The chapter opens with Blaine, Tracey, Summer, and Ulysses arriving back at Summer's underground lab in Alaska. They quickly begin learning about atoms and isotopes before Summer's old schoolmate, Paul Simms, interrupts with a call. They chat for a bit because Paul is trying to get information from Summer. After they hang up, we learn that Paul was behind the heist that the twins helped stop on their astronomy leg. It turns out that he had other plans and that he and the Rotary Club are working together on the moon! We head back to Summer's lab, where REESE shares a song about isotopes and the twins learn about elements before they prepare to head to the moon. Meanwhile, the Slote siblings, also known as the Rotary Club, arrive on the moon and make contact with Paul Simms. The chapter wraps up back in Switzerland, and Captain Marolf and his team get ready to support Summer on her mission to stop the Rotary Club on the moon!

Essential To-Do's

Read

- ☐ Read the section entitled "Atomic Bits" of Chapter 2 in *SSA Volume 7: Chemistry*.
- ☐ Read the section entitled "Dancing Elements" of Chapter 2 in *SSA Volume 7: Chemistry*.

Write

- ☐ Fill out a Chemistry Record Sheet on SL p. 9 on atoms.
- ☐ Fill out a Chemistry Record Sheet on SL p. 10 on elements.
- ☐ Fill out the lab report sheet for the demonstration on SL p. 13.
- ☐ Go over the vocabulary words and enter them into the Chemistry Glossary on SL pp. 102-103.

Do

- ☐ Do the demonstration entitled "Molecular Motion."

Optional Extras

Read

- ☐ Read one or all of the assigned pages from the encyclopedia of your choice.
- ☐ Read one of the additional library books.

Write

- ☐ Write a narration on the Chemistry Notes Sheet on SL p. 15.
- ☐ Complete the copywork or dictation assignment and add it to the Chemistry Notes Sheet on SL p. 15.
- ☐ Work on the Alaska Map Sheet on SL p. 17.
- ☐ Fill out the record sheet on SL p. 18 for one of the projects.

Do

- ☐ Make an Atom Model.
- ☐ Play the Atoms and Isotopes Game.

Supplies Needed	
Demo	• Jar with lid, Water, Food Coloring
Projects	• 4 Pipe cleaners, 9 Round beads in three different colors, at least 3 of each color • Atoms and Isotopes Game (free download from Elemental Science)

Chapter 2: 3...2...1...Chemistry

Read: Gathering Information

Living Book Spine
- Chapter 2 of *The Sassafras Science Adventures Volume 7: Chemistry*

(Optional) Encyclopedia Readings
- *DK Eyewitness: The Elements* pp. 4-5 (What is an element?), pp. 6-7 (Inside an atom)
- *Scholastic's The Periodic Table* pp. 8-9 (What is an element?)
- *Usborne Science Encyclopedia* pp. 10-11 (Atomic Structure), pp. 24-25 (The Elements)
- *Kingfisher Science Encyclopedia* pp. 148-149 (The Elements), pp. 150-151 (Atoms)

(Optional) Additional Library Books
- *What Are Atoms? (Rookie Read-About Science)* by Lisa Trumbauer
- *Atoms and Molecules (Building Blocks of Matter)* by Richard and Louise Spilsbury
- *Atoms (Simply Science)* by Melissa Stewart

Write: Keeping a Notebook

SCIDAT Logbook Sheets

This chapter, you can have the students work on the map sheet. You can also have them fill out the record sheets for atoms and elements along with adding to the notes sheet and glossary. The students should also complete a lab report sheet, and if they want, they can do a project record sheet. Here is the information they could include:

Alaska Map Sheet

This chapter, you can have the students look up the minerals found in Alaska. Here are a few possibilities:

- Zinc
- Gold
- Silver
- Cobalt
- Graphite
- Copper
- Rare Earth Elements (Lanthanum, Cerium, Gadolinium, Dysprosium, Holmium, Erbium, Ytterbium, Yttrium)

Here are two websites you can check out:

- https://www.blm.gov/programs/energy-and-minerals/mining-and-minerals/about/alaska
- https://www.usgs.gov/centers/national-minerals-information-center/mineral-industry-alaska

Chemistry Record Sheet - Atoms
INFORMATION LEARNED
- The Greeks were the first to discuss the concept of an atom. They believed that matter could be cut into smaller and smaller pieces but that eventually, you would get to a piece that could not be cut. So, the word atom comes from the Greek word, *atomos*, which means "uncuttable."
- It wasn't until 1808 that John Dalton, an English scientist and schoolteacher, developed a theory about how atoms behave. His theory said that an element is composed of tiny particles called atoms. In an ordinary chemical reaction, no atom of an element disappears, and compounds are formed when atoms of two or more elements combine.
- The modern atomic theory is similar to what Dalton proposed, except now we know the subparticles that compose an atom as well as that structure of an atom.
- The atom is composed of three smaller subatomic particles, called the proton, neutron, and electron.
    1. The proton is a positively charged particle that resides in the nucleus at the center of an atom.
    2. The neutron is a particle with no charge that also resides in the nucleus of an atom.
    3. The electron is a negatively charged particle that resides in a cloud around the nucleus, which is called an electron shell.
- Atoms have an equal number of protons and electrons, which gives them no net charge. In other words, the positive charges from the protons are canceled out by the negative charges of the electrons within the atom.
- Generally, an atom of a given element has the same number of neutrons as protons, but there are exceptions.

Chemistry Record Sheet - Elements
INFORMATION LEARNED
- Elements are substances made up of one type of atom that cannot be broken down by chemical reaction to form a simpler substance. In other words, they are a type of matter that cannot be broken down into two or more substances.
- There are 118 known elements at the time of this guide and 92 of them can be found naturally. The remainder must be synthetically produced, usually by man-made nuclear reactions.
- Each of the elements can be found arranged according to atomic number on the periodic table.

- Gold was one of the first elements to be discovered and used. It has been used for much of recorded history and was used extensively by the ancient Egyptians in the tombs of their pharaohs. The Bible records that Tubal-Cain used the element iron. However, the first concept of an element was described by the ancient Greek philosophers, who said that there were four elements: fire, earth, water, and air. They believed that all substances were a combination of these four elements.
- In 1661, Robert Boyle showed that there were more than the four classical elements, but it was not until 1789 that the first list of elements, which contained only 33 elements, was written by Antoine Lavoisier.
- In 1869, Dmitri Mendeleev was the first to organize the 66 known elements of his time into a

table that displayed the relationships between those elements. This table became the basis for our modern periodic table.
- As the field of science moved into the modern era, new instruments such as the spectroscope have allowed for more elements to be discovered.

Chemistry Notes - Isotopes

The following is information that the students could add to their notes page:
- Some atoms have additional neutrons in their nucleus, and we call these atoms isotopes of the element.
- These isotopes have the same atomic number, but different atomic mass. (**NOTE**—Remember that the atomic number is the number of protons in an element and atomic mass is the total weight of the protons, neutrons, and electrons in an element. So, it makes sense that an isotope would have the same atomic number, but a different atomic mass from the original element.)

Vocabulary

Have the older students look up the following terms in the glossary in the appendix on pp. 133-134 or in a science encyclopedia. Then, have them copy each definition onto a blank index card or into their SCIDAT logbook.

- ATOM – The tiny building blocks that make up everything in the universe.
- ELEMENT – A substance made up of one type of atom, which cannot be broken down by chemical reaction to form a simpler substance.
- ISOTOPE – An atom that has a different number of neutrons and so has a different mass number from the other atoms of an element.

(Optional) Copywork

Copywork Sentence

An element is made up of one or more of the same type of atom.

Dictation Selection

Elements are substances that are made up of one type of atom, whereas atoms are the smallest particles of an element that retain the chemical properties of the element. In other words, an element is made up of one or more of the same type of atom. So, when you hold a lump of iron ore, you are holding the element iron that contains billions of iron atoms.

Do: Playing with Science

Scientific Demonstration: Molecular Motion

Materials
- ☑ Jar with lid
- ☑ Water
- ☑ Food coloring

Procedure
1. Have the students fill the jar almost to the top with room-temperature water and drop several drops of

food coloring into the water.
2. Observe what happens within the first 30 seconds, asking them the following:

> **?** What is happening to the food coloring in the cup?

3. Then, have the students draw what they see in the box on the lab report sheet on SL p. 13.
4. Wait an hour, and have the students observe the jar again, asking them the following:

> **?** What has happened to the food coloring in the cup?

5. Then, have them draw what they see again in the box on the lab report sheet.

Explanation

The students should see the drops of food coloring moving through the water. After an hour, the whole cup will be full of colored water. This is because the atoms and molecules that make up these two liquids are in constant motion. Even though we can't see them moving, the water molecules are bumping into the food coloring molecules. Eventually, the two will be evenly mixed in the jar.

Take It Further

Have the students look at how temperature affects molecular motion by repeating the demonstration with a glass of ice-cold and hot-to-the-touch water. (The students should see that the food coloring molecules move much faster in the hot-to-the-touch water.)

(Optional) STEAM Projects

Multi-chapter Activities

✂ **Periodic Table Project** – Over the weeks of this study, the students will create a large, wall-sized periodic table or a small, lap-sized construction-paper version. This project will begin in Chapter 3.

Activities For This Chapter

✂ **Atom Model** – Have the students make a model of the atom using four pipe cleaners and nine round beads in three different colors with at least three of each color. Have the students select which beads will be electrons, protons, and neutrons. Next, have them string three protons beads and three neutrons beads on one of the pipe cleaners, alternating between the two. Once done, have the students wrap this portion of the pipe cleaner into a ball to form a nucleus, leaving a straight end to connect to the electron rings they will make in the next step. Then, have the students place one electron bead on a pipe cleaner and twist the pipe cleaner closed to form a ring. Repeat this process two more times so that they have three electron rings. Finally, fit the rings inside each other, and then hang the nucleus ball in the center, using the pipe cleaner tail left in step two to attach the nucleus and hold the rings together. (See image for reference.)

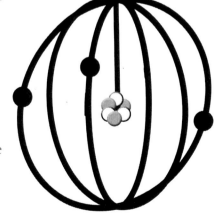

✂ **Atoms and Isotopes Game** – Have the students play the Atoms and Isotopes Game. You can get directions for this game from the following blog post:

🖱 http://elementalscience.com/blogs/science-activities/60317571-free-chemistry-game

Chapter 3: Grid Schedule

	Supplies Needed
Demo	• LEGO® bricks - a variety of colors and sizes (You can also used stuffed animals, buttons, beads, or any other object with different sizes and colors if you don't have any LEGO bricks.), Paper, Pen
Projects	• Red cabbage, Water, Pot, A variety of liquids or powders from your kitchen (such as lemon juice, baking soda, soda, or detergent), and Several cups

Chapter Summary

The chapter opens with Uncle Cecil reviewing what the twins learned about the periodic table along with an equation that he can't get off his mind—CS + SB -> L_2F_2. He realizes that Summer is becoming more than a good friend but wonders if she feels the same. We flash back to Blaine and Tracey as they are landing on the moon with Summer, Ulysses, and REESE. They take off for the stolen lunar module. Meanwhile, the Slote siblings are staking a claim for Paul Simms before they launch a rocket to take out a major satellite. At the same time, the twins have arrived at the lunar module and found tracks. Captain Marolf and his team help the group follow the tracks, and they soon find the infamous Rotary Club getting ready blow things up. Summer distracts them all with some information on hydrogen, while Blaine and Tracey get their TASER apps ready. The chapter ends with Tracey in position to stop the Rotary Club!

Weekly Schedule

	Day 1	Day 2	Day 3	Day 4
Read	☐ Read the section entitled "Periodic and Romantic Tables" of Chapter 3 in *SSA Volume 7: Chemistry*.	☐ Read the section entitled "Fueling Hydrogen" of Chapter 3 in *SSA Volume 7: Chemistry*.	☐ (*Optional*) Read one or all of the assigned pages from the encyclopedia of your choice.	☐ (*Optional*) Read one of the additional library books.
Write	☐ Fill out a Chemistry Record Sheet on SL p. 11 on the periodic table. ☐ Go over the vocabulary words and enter them into the Chemistry Glossary on SL p. 103.	☐ Fill out an Element Record Sheet on SL p. 12 on hydrogen. ☐ (*Optional*) Work on the Alaska Map Sheet on SL p. 17.	☐ (*Optional*) Write narration on the Chemistry Notes Sheet on SL p. 15. ☐ Fill out the lab report sheet for the demonstration on SL p. 13.	☐ (*Optional*) Complete the copywork or dictation assignment and add it to the Chemistry Notes Sheet on SL p. 15. ☐ (*Optional*) Fill out the record sheet on SL p. 14 for one of the projects. ☐ (*Optional*) Take Chemistry Quiz #1.
Do	☐ (*Optional*) Sing the Periodic Table Song.	☐ (*Optional*) Do the Kitchen Acid Test or the Hindenburg Hydogen Project.	☐ Do the demonstration entitled "Table Sorting."	☐ Work on the Periodic Table model.

Chapter 3: List Schedule

Chapter Summary

The chapter opens with Uncle Cecil reviewing what the twins learned about the periodic table along with an equation that he can't get off his mind—CS + SB -> L_2F_2. He realizes that Summer is becoming more than a good friend but wonders if she feels the same. We flash back to Blaine and Tracey as they are landing on the moon with Summer, Ulysses, and REESE. They take off for the stolen lunar module. Meanwhile, the Slote siblings are staking a claim for Paul Simms before they launch a rocket to take out a major satellite. At the same time, the twins have arrived at the lunar module and found tracks. Captain Marolf and his team help the group follow the tracks, and they soon find the infamous Rotary Club getting ready blow things up. Summer distracts them all with some information on hydrogen, while Blaine and Tracey get their TASER apps ready. The chapter ends with Tracey in position to stop the Rotary Club!

Essential To-Do's

Read
- ☐ Read the section entitled "Periodic and Romantic Tables" of Chapter 3 in *SSA Volume 7: Chemistry*.
- ☐ Read the section entitled "Fueling Hydrogen" of Chapter 3 in *SSA Volume 7: Chemistry*.

Write
- ☐ Fill out a Chemistry Record Sheet on SL p. 11 on the periodic table.
- ☐ Fill out an Element Record Sheet on SL p. 12 on hydrogen.
- ☐ Fill out the lab report sheet for the demonstration on SL p. 13.
- ☐ Go over the vocabulary word and enter it into the Chemistry Glossary on SL p. 103.

Do
- ☐ Do the demonstration entitled "Table Sorting."
- ☐ Work on the Periodic Table model.

Optional Extras

Read
- ☐ Read one or all of the assigned pages from the encyclopedia of your choice.
- ☐ Read one of the additional library books.

Write
- ☐ Write a narration on the Chemistry Notes Sheet on SL p. 15.
- ☐ Complete the copywork or dictation assignment and add it to the Chemistry Notes Sheet on SL p. 15.
- ☐ Fill out the record sheet on SL p. 14 for one of the projects.
- ☐ Work on the Alaska Map Sheet on SL p. 17.
- ☐ Take Chemistry Quiz #1.

Do
- ☐ Sing the Periodic Table Song.
- ☐ Do the Kitchen Acid Test or the Hindenburg Hydogen Project.

	Supplies Needed
Demo	• LEGO® bricks - a variety of colors and sizes (you can also used stuffed animals, buttons, beads, or any other object with different sizes and colors if you don't have any LEGO bricks), Paper, Pen
Projects	• Red cabbage, Water, Pot, A variety of liquids or powders from your kitchen (such as lemon juice, baking soda, soda, or detergent), and Several cups

Chapter 3: Launching Lunar Adventures

Read: Gathering Information

Living Book Spine
- Chapter 3 of *The Sassafras Science Adventures Volume 7: Chemistry*

(Optional) Encyclopedia Readings
- *DK Eyewitness: The Elements* pp. 8-9 (The periodic table), pp. 12-13 (Hydrogen)
- *Scholastic's The Periodic Table* pp. 14-15 (The Periodic Table), pp. 20-21 (Hydrogen)
- *Usborne Science Encyclopedia* pp. 28-29 (The Periodic Table), pp. 84-85 (Acids and Bases)
- *Kingfisher Science Encyclopedia* pp. 152-153 (The Periodic Table), p. 184 (Acids), p. 185 (Bases and Alkalis)

(Optional) Additional Library Books
- *The Mystery of the Periodic Table (Living History Library)* by Benjamin D. Wiker, Jeanne Bendick, and Theodore Schluenderfritz
- *The Periodic Table (True Books: Elements)* by Salvatore Tocci
- *Hydrogen and the Noble Gases (True Books: Elements)* by Salvatore Tocci
- *Hydrogen: Running on Water (Energy Revolution)* by Niki Walker

Write: Keeping a Notebook

SCIDAT Logbook Sheets

This chapter, you can have the students finish the map sheet. You can also have them fill out the record sheets for the periodic table and hydrogen, along with adding to the notes sheet and glossary. The students should also complete a lab report sheet, and if they want, they can do a project record sheet. Here is the information they could include:

Alaska Map Sheet

This chapter, you can have the students look up the industry found in Alaska. Here are a few possibilities:

- Oil
- Gas

Here are pages from the suggested atlas you can read:
- *DK Children's Illustrated Atlas* pp. 12-13 (Canada and Alaska)

Chemistry Record Sheet - The Periodic Table
Information Learned
- The periodic table is a systematic arrangement of the elements in order of increasing atomic number. It is designed to group elements with similar properties together.

- The periodic table gives the following information for each element:
  1. The atomic number, which is the number of protons that can be found in the nucleus of an atom.
  2. The atomic mass, which is the total weight of the protons, neutrons, and electrons in each atom. Sometimes this can vary if there are isotopes of the element, so the atomic mass given on the periodic table is an average of those varying weights.
  3. The symbol, which is the one-, two-, or three-letter code that scientists use for the element. This code is accepted internationally to remove language barriers when discussing chemical compounds. Some are easy, like O for oxygen; some make less sense, like Pb for lead. This is because the symbol is typically based on the Latin name for the element, which in the case of lead is *plumbum*. Chemists use the symbol of an element when referring to it in a compound or equation, so these are important to know.
- As you move from left to right on the table, the atomic number and atomic mass of the element increases. The same is true as you travel down the periodic table.
- The original periodic table was created by Russian chemist Dmitri Mendeleev.
- Even though our modern-day table looks quite a bit different from what Mendeleev drew, we still give him credit for the original idea of the periodic table.

Element Record Sheet - Hydrogen

GROUP NAME: Alkali Metal

INFORMATION LEARNED

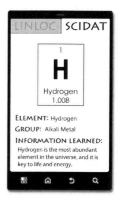

- Hydrogen is the first element on the periodic table. As such, the normal state of the hydrogen atom has one proton and one neutron in the nucleus and one electron soaring around the nucleus.
- It is the most abundant element in the universe, and it is key to energy and life.
- Hydrogen is the fuel that makes it possible for the Sun to burn brightly.
- On Earth, it exists as a gas, which consists of a pair of hydrogen atoms (H_2).
- Hydrogen gas is extremely flammable. But it is lighter than air and can escape the Earth's atmosphere. It was used to fill airships until the Hindenburg disaster.
- Hydrogen on Earth is also found bonded to other elements in compounds such as water, hydrocarbons, acids, and bases.
- At low temperature and high pressure, hydrogen gas becomes a liquid.
- These days, hydrogen is being looked at as an option for a clean and efficient fuel cell. There are several new cars that use this technology. In these vehicles, inside the fuel cell, hydrogen and oxygen combine to form water and produce electricity and heat. The main problem with these fuel cells is the volatility of hydrogen.
- Hydrogen is also used in fertilizers, in oil refining, in welding, in nuclear fusion, and as rocket fuel.

Chemistry Notes - Acids and Bases

The following is information that the students could add to their notes page:
- Acids are chemicals that dissolve in water and can neutralize a base. Acids are hydrogen-containing compounds that split up in water to give hydrogen ions. Weak acids taste sour.

- Bases are chemicals that dissolve in water and can neutralize an acid. Bases are compounds that react with an acid to produce water and a salt. Weak bases taste bitter.

VOCABULARY

Have the older students look up the following terms in the glossary in the appendix on pp. 133-134 or in a science encyclopedia. Then, have them copy each definition onto a blank index card or into their SCIDAT logbook.

- ATOMIC NUMBER – The number of protons in the nucleus of an atom.
- ATOMIC MASS – The average mass number of the atoms in a sample of an element.
- CHEMICAL SYMBOL – A shorthand way of representing a specific element in formulae and equations.

(OPTIONAL) COPYWORK

Copywork Sentence

The periodic table is logical layout of the elements in order of increasing atomic number.

Dictation Selection (excerpt from the Periodic Table Poem, author unknown)

Each element has a spot on the periodic table,
Whether metal or gas, radioactive or stable.
You can find out its number, its symbol, its weight,
And from its position, its physical state.

(OPTIONAL) QUIZ

This chapter, you can give the students a quiz based on what they learned in Chapters 2 and 3. You can find the quiz in the appendix on p. 143.

Quiz #1 Answers
1. A,D,E,F,B,C
2. Positive, Negative, Neutral
3. True
4. True
5. False (An element is made up of one single type of atom.)
6. Gas
7. Bitter, Sour

DO: PLAYING WITH SCIENCE

SCIENTIFIC DEMONSTRATION: TABLE SORTING

Materials
- ☑ LEGO® bricks - a variety of colors and sizes (you can also used stuffed animals, buttons, beads, or any other object with different sizes and colors if you don't have any LEGO bricks)
- ☑ Paper
- ☑ Pen

Procedure
1. Gather the LEGO bricks in an unorganized pile. Draw a four-by-six grid on the piece of paper. If

you are using larger objects to sort, such as stuffed animals, you can create this grid on the floor with masking tape. Say the following to the students:

> We are going to make a periodic table of (objects you are using). In this table, the (objects you are using) are going to get bigger as you go down the grid and darker as you go across.

	White	Yellow	Red	Blue	Brown	Black
smallest						
largest						

See the included grid for visual explanation.

2. Have the students sort the objects by size and color onto the grid. As they sort, share with them how the periodic table in chemistry is an organized assortment of elements set up in a grid, similar to how they are sorting their objects.
3. Have the students complete the lab report on SL p. 14.

Explanation

The point of this demonstrations is for the students to see the order that exists in the arrangement of the elements in the periodic table.

Take It Further

Have the students create another table for different objects.

(Optional) STEAM Projects

Multi-chapter Activities

✂ **Periodic Table Project** – This chapter, the students will begin their large, wall-sized periodic table or a small, lap-sized construction-paper version. Have the students draw the outline of the periodic table on a sheet of paper, or use full table found on SL p. 5. They will begin to add groups next week.

Activities For This Chapter

✂ **Periodic Table Song** – Have the students listen to the Periodic Table Song as many times as they need to until they are able to memorize the elements:

🖱 https://www.youtube.com/watch?v=rz4Dd1I_fX0

You can also use flash cards to help memorize the elements of the periodic table.

✂ **Kitchen Acid Test** – Have the students test kitchen materials for acids and bases. You will need a head of red cabbage, water, pot, several cups, and a variety of liquids or powders from your kitchen to test, such as lemon juice, baking soda, soda, or detergent. You can find the directions for this project here:

🖱 https://elementalscience.com/blogs/science-activities/kitchen-acid-test

✂ **Hindenburg Hydrogen** – Have the students learn about the Hindenburg, which was an air ship filled with hydrogen. You can read the following books with your students:

📖 *You Wouldn't Want to Be on the Hindenburg!* by Ian Graham
📖 *The Hindenburg Disaster (True Books: Disasters)* by Peter Benoit

Please preview these books to make sure that they are appropriate for your students.

Chapter 4: Grid Schedule

	Supplies Needed
Demo	• 3 Cups, Water, Food coloring, Salt
Projects	• Cup, Baking Soda, Vinegar • Coffee filter, Rubbing alcohol, Eyedropper, Jar, Rubber band, Permanent markers in a variety of colors • Heavy cream, Milk, Sugar, Vanilla, 1 quart-sized Ziploc plastic baggie, Crushed ice, 1 gallon-sized Ziploc plastic baggie, Rock salt

Chapter Summary

The chapter opens in Switzerland, where we see that Summer and her team have defeated the Rotary Club on the moon! Back in Alaska, we learn a bit more about what happened on the moon and what will happen to the Slote siblings. After an awkward conversation with Paul Sims, Summer says goodbye to the twins, and they head to Siberia. They land in a large mining truck where they soon witness an exchange between two miners and two consultants about whether the mining operation needs more science and joviality. The twins learn about alkali metals, sodium, and potassium while they sit inside of the truck as they listen to Rodi and Dina Abramov's plan. The two miners, Trof and Taras, feel differently about the upcoming changes. Trof storms off, taking Taras with him, but not before he dumps the entire load from the back of the truck, a load that includes the Sassafras twins, at the Abramov's feet. The chapter ends with a flash to the Man With No Eyebrows where we learn of his plan to erase the memories of up to 20 people at one time with his latest machine!

Weekly Schedule

	Day 1	Day 2	Day 3	Day 4
Read	☐ Read the section entitled "Abundant Alkali" of Chapter 4 in *SSA Volume 7: Chemistry*.	☐ Read the section entitled "Shiny Sodium and Purply Potassium" of Chapter 4 in *SSA Volume 7: Chemistry*.	☐ *(Optional)* Read one or all of the assigned pages from the encyclopedia of your choice.	☐ *(Optional)* Read one of the additional library books.
Write	☐ Fill out the Periodic Table Group Sheet on SL p. 20 on alkali metals. ☐ Go over the vocabulary words and enter them into the Chemistry Glossary on SL p. 104.	☐ Fill out an Element Record Sheet on SL p. 21 on sodium. ☐ Fill out an Element Record Sheet on SL p. 22 on potassium. ☐ *(Optional)* Work on the Siberia Map Sheet on SL p. 30.	☐ *(Optional)* Write narration on the Chemistry Notes Sheet on SL p. 28. ☐ Fill out the lab report sheet for the demonstration on SL p. 26.	☐ *(Optional)* Complete the copywork or dictation assignment and add it to the Chemistry Notes Sheet on SL p. 28. ☐ *(Optional)* Fill out the record sheet on SL p. 31 for one of the projects.
Do	☐ *(Optional)* Make an Ice Cream Mixture.	☐ *(Optional)* Do the Sodium Reaction or do some Marker Chromatography.	☐ Do the demonstration entitled "Which one freezes first?"	☐ Work on the Periodic Table model.

Chapter 4: List Schedule

Chapter Summary

The chapter opens in Switzerland, where we see that Summer and her team have defeated the Rotary Club on the moon! Back in Alaska, we learn a bit more about what happened on the moon and what will happen to the Slote siblings. After an awkward conversation with Paul Sims, Summer says goodbye to the twins, and they head to Siberia. They land in a large mining truck where they soon witness an exchange between two miners and two consultants about whether the mining operation needs more science and joviality. The twins learn about alkali metals, sodium, and potassium while they sit inside of the truck as they listen to Rodi and Dina Abramov's plan. The two miners, Trof and Taras, feel differently about the upcoming changes. Trof storms off, taking Taras with him, but not before he dumps the entire load from the back of the truck, a load that includes the Sassafras twins, at the Abramov's feet. The chapter ends with a flash to the Man With No Eyebrows where we learn of his plan to erase the memories of up to 20 people at one time with his latest machine!

Essential To-Do's

Read
- ☐ Read the section entitled "Abundant Alkali" of Chapter 4 in *SSA Volume 7: Chemistry*.
- ☐ Read the section entitled "Shiny Sodium and Purply Potassium" of Chapter 4 in *SSA Volume 7: Chemistry*.

Write
- ☐ Fill out the Periodic Table Group Sheet on SL p. 20 on alkali metals.
- ☐ Fill out an Element Record Sheet on SL p. 21 on sodium.
- ☐ Fill out an Element Record Sheet on SL p. 22 on potassium.
- ☐ Fill out the lab report sheet for the demonstration on SL p. 26.
- ☐ Go over the vocabulary words and enter them into the Chemistry Glossary on SL p. 104.

Do
- ☐ Do the demonstration entitled "Which one freezes first?"
- ☐ Work on the Periodic Table model.

Optional Extras

Read
- ☐ Read one or all of the assigned pages from the encyclopedia of your choice.
- ☐ Read one of the additional library books.

Write
- ☐ Write a narration on the Chemistry Notes Sheet on SL p. 28.
- ☐ Complete the copywork or dictation assignment and add it to the Chemistry Notes Sheet on SL p. 28.
- ☐ Fill out the record sheet on SL p. 31 for one of the projects.
- ☐ Work on the Siberia Map Sheet on SL p. 30.

Do
- ☐ Make an Ice Cream Mixture.
- ☐ Do the Sodium Reaction.
- ☐ Do some Marker Chromatography.

	Supplies Needed
Demo	• 3 Cups, Water, Food coloring, Salt
Projects	• Cup, Baking Soda, Vinegar • Coffee filter, Rubbing alcohol, Eyedropper, Jar, Rubber band, Permanent markers in a variety of colors • Heavy cream, Milk, Sugar, Vanilla, 1 quart-sized Ziploc plastic baggie, Crushed ice, 1 gallon-sized Ziploc plastic baggie, Rock salt

Chapter 4: Underground Siberian Science...

Read: Gathering Information

Living Book Spine

- Chapter 4 of *The Sassafras Science Adventures Volume 7: Chemistry*

(Optional) Encyclopedia Readings

- *DK Eyewitness: The Elements* pp. 14-17 (Alkali Metals)
- *Scholastic's The Periodic Table* pp. 24-25 (Alkali Metals), pp. 28-29 (Sodium), p. 33 (Potassium)
- *Usborne Science Encyclopedia* pp. 60-61 (Separating Mixtures)
- *Kingfisher Science Encyclopedia* pp. 160-161 (Separation and Purification)

(Optional) Additional Library Books

- *The Alkali Metals: Lithium, Sodium, Potassium, Rubidium, Cesium, Francium (Understanding the Elements of the Periodic Table)* by Kristi Lew
- *Sodium (Elements)* by Anne O'Daly
- *Sodium (True Books: Elements)* by Salvatore Tocci
- *Potassium (Elements)* by Chris Woodford
- *Mix It Up! Solution or Mixture?* by Tracy Nelson Maurer

Write: Keeping a Notebook

SCIDAT Logbook Sheets

This chapter, you can have the students work on the map sheet. You can also have them fill out the record sheets for alkali metals, sodium, and potassium along with adding to the notes sheet and glossary. The students should also complete a lab report sheet, and if they want, they can do a project record sheet. Here is the information they could include:

Siberia Map Sheet

This chapter, you can have the students look up the minerals found in Siberia. Here are a few possibilities:

- Iron
- Gold
- Aluminum
- Copper
- Uranium
- Lead
- Zinc
- Bauxite
- Nickel
- Tin
- Mercury
- Silver

Here are several websites you can check out:

- https://www.britannica.com/place/Siberia

- https://www.mining-technology.com/features/siberia-will-frozen-wilderness-give-riches/
- https://factsanddetails.com/russia/Economics_Business_Agriculture/sub9_7e/entry-5176.html

Periodic Table Group Sheet - Alkali Metals

Elements Included
- Sodium
- Potassium
- Lithium
- Rubidium
- Cesium
- Francium

Interesting Information
- Alkali metals are so reactive because they want to bond with other elements so they can get rid of the one electron that sits in the outer shell.
- As you go down the group on the periodic table, the more reactive the metal gets, so cesium is way more reactive than lithium.
- These metals are soft and shiny, but they change color as soon as they hit the air.
- Lithium is the lightest metal on the periodic table, and it has many uses from batteries to light-weight metal alloys for aircraft to absorbing carbon dioxide from the air that astronauts breathe.
- Rubidium has such a low melting point that it will melt in your hand, but a compound including this metal, rubidium nitrate, gives the purple color to fireworks.
- Cesium is so reactive that it explodes in water, but it is used to keep clocks accurate.
- Francium is the rarest natural element on Earth. It has no practical uses because it is so rare and because it decays so quickly.

Element Record Sheet - Sodium

Group Name: Alkali Metal

Information Learned
- Sodium is a soft, silvery metal that is so light that it can flow on water.
- The symbol for sodium is Na. The atomic number for sodium is 11 and the atomic mass is 22.99.
- The pure metal will burst into flames when it touches water.
- Sodium reacts quickly with chlorine to form sodium chloride, also known as table salt.
- This sodium salt is one of the only rocks we humans eat—it can be mined as rock salt or produced by the evaporation of seawater.
- Humans have just under 9 oz of sodium chloride in their bodies, which helps transmit nerve signals around the body. Because we sweat out salt, we need to constantly replace the sodium chloride through our diet.

Element Record Sheet - Potassium

Group Name: Alkali Metal

Information Learned
- The symbol for potassium is K. The atomic number for potassium is 19 and the atomic mass is 39.10.
- Potassium is a soft metal that burns with a lilac flame when it hits water.
- Potassium turns black in the open air.
- Potassium is essential to life as it helps maintain the health of our cells and blood vessels. This element also works with sodium to conduct electrical

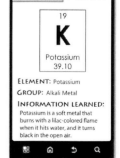

signals around the body for muscle contraction.
- Humans can't make potassium so we have to get it through our diet.
- Potassium is also necessary for plants, and it is often used as a fertilizer.

Chemistry Notes - Mixtures

The following is information that the students could add to their notes page:
- Mixtures are a combination of two or more elements that are not chemically bonded together. Air is a mixture of gases. Seawater is a mixture of water and salts. Soil is a mixture of different solids.
- All mixtures can be separated into their components using techniques like decantation, filtration, chromatography, evaporation, distillation, or centrifugation.

Vocabulary

Have the older students look up the following terms in the glossary in the appendix on pp. 133-134 or in a science encyclopedia. Then, have them copy each definition onto a blank index card or into their SCIDAT logbook.

- MIXTURE – A combination of two or more elements that are not chemically bonded together.
- REACTIVE – The tendency of a substance to react with other substances.

(Optional) Copywork

Copywork Sentence

Alkali metals are soft and shiny. These metals change color as soon as they hit the air.

Dictation Selection

Alkali metals are very reactive elements. These metals want to bond with other elements so they can get rid of the one electron that sits in their outer shell. As you go down the group on the periodic table, the more reactive the alkali metal gets. This means that cesium is way more reactive than lithium.

Do: Playing with Science

Scientific Demonstration: Which One Freezes First

Materials
- 3 Cups
- Water
- Food coloring
- Salt
- Instant-read thermometer

Procedure

1. Have the students begin by labeling the cups #1 to #3. Then, add a half cup of water to each of the cups.
2. Next, do the following:
   - To cup #1, add several drops of food coloring and mix well.
   - To cup #2, add one tablespoon of salt and stir until completely dissolved.
   - To cup #3, add nothing.
3. Have the students take the initial temperature of the cups and place each one in the freezer.

4. Over the next 2 hours, have them check the cups every 30 minutes to observe what is happening and take the temperature of each cup. Each time, have the students record the temperature in the box on the lab report sheet on SL p. 26.
5. After 2 hours, have them add their final observations to the lab report.

Explanation

The students should see that cup #1 and cup #2 freeze at the same time, whereas cup #3 takes quite a bit longer to freeze. In fact they may see that cup #3 does not even freeze in the allotted 3 hours. The students should see that all three cups were around the same temperature each time. This is because salt, which is sodium chloride, lowers the freezing point of water. This means that water with salt in it will remain a liquid for longer than plain water because the point at which salt water will freeze is lower than 32°F. Food coloring has no effect on the freezing temperature of water, so it will freeze at the same temperature as the plain water.

Take It Further

Once all of your cups have frozen, have the students take them out of the freezer and see which one melts the quickest. You can do this by setting each cup on the counter or by heating them in a pan. The students should see that cup #3 (the one with the salt) melts quicker for the same reasons in the explanation. This is why we use salt to melt ice on the driveway during the winter.

(Optional) STEAM Projects

Multi-chapter Activities

- **Periodic Table Project** – This chapter, the students will add the alkali metals on SL p. 111 to their periodic table poster on SL p. 5.

Activities For This Chapter

- **Sodium Reaction** – Have the students learn about the chemistry of another sodium compound in your kitchen, baking soda, aka sodium bicarbonate. Add 1 tablespoon of baking soda to a cup. Then, have the students add a few drops of white vinegar and observe what happens! (This is the classic acid [vinegar] and base [baking soda] reaction. If you already did this experiment as part of the "Take It Further" option in Chapter 1, this time you can share a more detailed explanation of what is happening. In this reaction, the bubbles you see are a release of the energy and the products from the reaction—carbon dioxide gas, sodium acetate, and water.)

- **Marker Chromatography** – Have the students learn more about separating mixtures through chromatography. You will need coffee filters, rubbing alcohol, an eyedropper, a jar, rubber band, and permanent markers in a variety of colors. The directions for this activity can be found here:
    - https://elementalscience.com/blogs/science-activities/marker-chromatography-steam-activity

- **Ice Cream Mixture** – Have the students make a frozen solution—ice cream in a bag! You will need ½ cup of heavy cream, ½ cup of milk, 1 tablespoon of sugar, ½ teaspoon of vanilla, 1 quart-size Ziploc plastic bag, 2 cups of crushed ice, 1 gallon-size Ziploc plastic bag, and ½ cup of rock salt. Begin by adding the cream, milk, sugar, and vanilla to the quart-size baggie, close it, and shake vigorously to mix well. Then, add the ice and rock salt to the gallon-size baggie, mix well, and then nestle the quart-size bag into the ice mixture. Seal the large baggie tightly, and begin shaking! (NOTE—It will take about 10 to 15 minutes for ice cream to form. You can use a towel or oven mitt to hold the large baggie as you shake if it gets too cold to handle.)

Chapter 5: Grid Schedule

	Supplies Needed
Demo	• Epsom salts, Ammonia, Water, Clear cup
Projects	• Egg, White vinegar, Clear Glass • Pot, Water, Green veggie of your choice, Baking soda

Chapter Summary

The chapter opens with Blaine letting us know about his secret dream to be a break-dancer, a dream that he hopes will be fulfilled at that night's talent show and concert in the underground mine. The twins get a tour of the changes to the underground mining chamber from the Abramovs, and Rodi shares with them about alkaline earth metals. The twins then learn that their old friend from their botany leg, Svetta Corvetta, will be performing at the concert with her band Sveta and the Spark Plugs. We flip between locations, learning that the Man With No Eyebrows is ready to unleash his Forget-O-Nator bus and that Uncle Cecil is getting ready for a special dinner, all while the concert preparations are fully underway in the mine. We also learn more of the story of how the Man With No Eyebrows lost his eyebrows to a freak Bunsen burner accident way back in middle school. Flash back to the twins in the underground mine, where they learn about magnesium and calcium as the final preparations are being made for the talent show and concert. The talent show begins, and in the middle of the first act, a continuous miner comes barreling into the room. It's driven remotely by the miner Trof, and he angrily destroys what is in its path. The chapter ends with Trof and a group of dust-colored miners facing off with Sveta and the neon-clad miners.

Weekly Schedule

	Day 1	Day 2	Day 3	Day 4
Read	☐ Read the section entitled "Extravagant Earth Metals" of Chapter 5 in *SSA Volume 7: Chemistry*.	☐ Read the section entitled "Magnesium and Calcium Mash-up" of Chapter 5 in *SSA Volume 7: Chemistry*.	☐ *(Optional)* Read one or all of the assigned pages from the encyclopedia of your choice.	☐ *(Optional)* Read one of the additional library books.
Write	☐ Fill out the Periodic Table Group Sheet on SL p. 23 on alkaline earth metals. ☐ Go over the vocabulary word and enter it into the Chemistry Glossary on SL p. 104.	☐ Fill out an Element Record Sheet on SL p. 24 on magnesium. ☐ Fill out an Element Record Sheet on SL p. 25 on calcium. ☐ *(Optional)* Work on the Siberia Map Sheet on SL p. 30.	☐ *(Optional)* Write narration on the Chemistry Notes Sheet on SL p. 29. ☐ Fill out the lab report sheet for the demonstration on SL p. 27.	☐ *(Optional)* Complete the copywork or dictation assignment and add it to the Chemistry Notes Sheet on SL p. 29. ☐ *(Optional)* Fill out the record sheet on SL p. 32 for one of the projects. ☐ *(Optional)* Take Chemistry Quiz #2.
Do	☐ *(Optional)* Watch the Alkaline Earth Metals video.	☐ *(Optional)* Do the Dissolving Calcium or make Magnesium Veggies.	☐ Do the demonstration entitled "Magnesium Solutions."	☐ Work on the Periodic Table model.

Chapter 5: List schedule

Chapter Summary

The chapter opens with Blaine letting us know about his secret dream to be a break-dancer, a dream that he hopes will be fulfilled at that night's talent show and concert in the underground mine. The twins get a tour of the changes to the underground mining chamber from the Abramovs, and Rodi shares with them about alkaline earth metals. The twins then learn that their old friend from their botany leg, Svetta Corvetta, will be performing at the concert with her band Sveta and the Spark Plugs. We flip between locations, learning that the Man With No Eyebrows is ready to unleash his Forget-O-Nator bus and that Uncle Cecil is getting ready for a special dinner, all while the concert preparations are fully underway in the mine. We also learn more of the story of how the Man With No Eyebrows lost his eyebrows to a freak Bunsen burner accident way back in middle school. Flash back to the twins in the underground mine, where they learn about magnesium and calcium as the final preparations are being made for the talent show and concert. The talent show begins, and in the middle of the first act, a continuous miner comes barreling into the room. It's driven remotely by the miner Trof, and he angrily destroys what is in its path. The chapter ends with Trof and a group of dust-colored miners facing off with Sveta and the neon-clad miners.

Essential To-Do's

Read
- ☐ Read the section entitled "Extravagant Earth Metals" of Chapter 5 in *SSA Volume 7: Chemistry*.
- ☐ Read the section entitled "Magnesium and Calcium Mash-up" of Chapter 5 in *SSA Volume 7: Chemistry*.

Write
- ☐ Fill out the Periodic Table Group Sheet on SL p. 23 on alkaline earth metals.
- ☐ Fill out an Element Record Sheet on SL p. 24 on magnesium.
- ☐ Fill out an Element Record Sheet on SL p. 25 on calcium.
- ☐ Fill out the lab report sheet for the demonstration on SL p. 27.
- ☐ Go over the vocabulary word and enter it into the Chemistry Glossary on SL p. 104.

Do
- ☐ Do the demonstration entitled "Magnesium Solutions."
- ☐ Work on the Periodic Table model.

Optional Extras

Read
- ☐ Read one or all of the assigned pages from the encyclopedia of your choice.
- ☐ Read one of the additional library books.

Write
- ☐ Write a narration on the Chemistry Notes Sheet on SL p. 29.
- ☐ Complete the copywork or dictation assignment and add it to the Chemistry Notes Sheet on SL p. 29.
- ☐ Fill out the record sheet on SL p. 32 for one of the projects.
- ☐ Work on the Siberia Map Sheet on SL p. 30.
- ☐ Take Chemistry Quiz #2.

Do
- ☐ Watch the Alkaline Earth Metals video.
- ☐ Do the Dissolving Calcium or make Magnesium Veggies.

Supplies Needed	
Demo	• Epsom salts, Ammonia, Water, Clear cup
Projects	• Egg, White vinegar, Clear Glass • Pot, Water, Green veggie of your choice, Baking soda

Chapter 5: Subterranean Dance-off

Read: Gathering Information

Living Book Spine

📖 Chapter 5 of *The Sassafras Science Adventures Volume 7: Chemistry*

(Optional) Encyclopedia Readings

🔍 *DK Eyewitness: The Elements* pp. 18-21 (Alkaline Earth Metals)
🔍 *Scholastic's The Periodic Table* pp. 34-35 (Alkaline Earth Metals), p. 37 (Magnesium), pp. 40-41 (Calcium)
🔍 *Usborne Science Encyclopedia* pp. 58-59 (Mixtures)
🔍 *Kingfisher Science Encyclopedia* pp. 158-159 (Solutions)

(Optional) Additional Library Books

📖 *The Alkaline Earth Metals: Beryllium, Magnesium, Calcium, Strontium, Barium, Radium (Understanding the Elements of the Periodic Table)* by Bridget Heos
📖 *Calcium (True Books: Elements)* by Salvatore Tocci
📖 *Magnesium (The Elements)* by Colin Uttley
📖 *Mixtures and Solutions (Building Blocks of Matter)* by Richard Spilsbury and Louise Spilsbury

Write: Keeping a Notebook

SCIDAT Logbook Sheets

This chapter, you can have the students finish the map sheet. You can also have them fill out the record sheets for alkaline earth metals, magnesium, and calcium along with adding to the notes sheet and glossary. The students should also complete a lab report sheet, and if they want, they can do a project record sheet. Here is the information they could include:

Siberia Map Sheet

This chapter, you can have the students look up the industry found in Siberia. Here are a few possibilities:

- Oil
- Gas
- Coal
- Rubber
- Fertilizer
- Nitric and Sulfuric Acids

Here are pages from the suggested atlas you can read:

📖 *DK Children's Illustrated Atlas* pp. 84-85 (Asian Russia and Kazakhstan)

Periodic Table Group Sheet - Alkaline Earth Metals

Elements Included

- Beryllium
- Magnesium
- Calcium
- Strontium

- Barium
- Radium

Interesting Information
- The alkaline earth metals are a little less reactive than the alkali metals next to them because they have two electrons in their outer shells.
- They combine easily with oxygen to form many of the minerals found in the Earth's crust.
- All six alkaline earth metals are good conductors of heat and electricity.
- Only magnesium and calcium are essential to life.
- On their own, the alkaline earth metals are shiny, slivery-gray, and lightweight metals.
- Beryllium is the key element in the mineral beryl, which gives many gemstones their green color, such as emeralds, aquamarine, and morganite.
- Strontium burns red and is used in road flares. It is toxic in high levels, but small amounts of it are used in toothpaste.
- Barium gives fireworks their green color, plus it is used in glassmaking and in X-rays because a compound containing barium glows under X-ray light.
- Radium was once thought of as a miracle metal because it gave off heat and light, but nowadays we know that it is radioactive and can cause cancer.

Element Record Sheet - Magnesium

Group Name: Alkaline Earth Metal

Information Learned
- The symbol for magnesium is Mg. The atomic number for magnesium is 12 and the atomic mass is 24.31.
- Magnesium is the third-most abundant element in seawater.
- Magnesium is an essential element to life. It helps plants make their food, and it aids in more than 300 functions in the body.
- Magnesium is also used as part of the metal alloy in materials used to build airplanes and cars.
- When magnesium is burned, it burns with an intensely white flame.

Element Record Sheet - Calcium

Group Name: Alkaline Earth Metal

Information Learned
- The symbol for calcium is Ca. The atomic number for calcium is 20 and the atomic mass is 40.08.
- Calcium is essential to human life because it is part of what gives our teeth and bones their strength.
- Calcium is sometimes referred to as the "scaffolder" element because its effect is often to hold things together, such as in bones, rocks, shells, and cement.
- Calcium can be found in marble, limestone, and chalk.
- Calcium will dissolve in water, causing the water to be considered hard water. When the water evaporates, the calcium is left behind, forming lime scale.

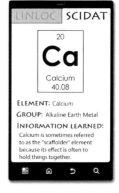

Chemistry Notes - Solutions

The following is information that the students could add to their notes page:

- A solution is a type of mixture that consists of a solid substance, called the solute, dissolved in a liquid, called the solvent.
- If the solid dissolves easily in the solvent, it is said to be soluble. If the solid does not dissolve in the solvent, it is said to be insoluble.
- Soluble solutions can typically be separated by chromatography, evaporation, or distillation.

Vocabulary

Have the older students look up the following term in the glossary in the appendix on pp. 133-134 or in a science encyclopedia. Then, have them copy each definition onto a blank index card or into their SCIDAT logbook.

SOLUTION – A mixture that consists of a substance dissolved in a liquid.

(Optional) Copywork

Copywork Sentence

Magnesium and calcium are essential elements to life.

Dictation Selection

Alkali metals and alkaline earth metals are essential to life. Sodium helps transmit nerve signals around the body. Potassium helps maintain the health of our cells and blood vessels. Magnesium helps plants make their food. Calcium gives our teeth and bones their strength.

(Optional) Quiz

This chapter, you can give the students a quiz based on what they learned in Chapters 4 and 5. You can find the quiz in the appendix on p. 145.

Quiz #2 Answers

1. B,A,C
2. True
3. Sodium
4. False (Humans can't make potassium, so we have to get it through our diet.)
5. Students' answers can include the following: soft metals; often bonded to oxygen; react easily
6. False (Magnesium is a solid metal that burns with a bright white light.)
7. Students' answers can include the following: bones, teeth, hard water, limestone, cement, and chalk
8. Are not

Do: Playing with Science

Scientific Demonstration: Magnesium Solutions

Materials
- ☑ Epsom salts
- ☑ Ammonia
- ☑ Water

☑ Clear cup

Procedure
1. Have the students fill the cup about halfway with warm water.
2. Then, add a teaspoon of Epsom salts and stir until it's dissolved.
3. Next, pour in 2 teaspoons of ammonia, but DO NOT stir.
4. Let the jar sit for 5 minutes, and observe what happens.
5. Have the students draw what they see in the box on the lab report sheet on SL p. 27.

Explanation

The students should see a milky, white substance within 5 minutes. This substance is magnesium hydroxide, which does not dissolve in water. This is a compound of an alkaline earth metal, magnesium. (NOTE—If the cup sits undisturbed for about 30 minutes longer, the white substance will settle out on top of the water layer.)

Take It Further

Have the students make another magnesium solution that forms crystals. You will need Epsom salts, water, and a small jar. Have the students mix a third of a cup of Epsom salts with a half of a cup of warm water. Stir to dissolve, and place the jar in the refrigerator where it can sit undisturbed. Check the jar after a few hours, and observe what has happened. (The students should see crystals have formed at the bottom of the jar. These are magnesium sulfate crystals, which are the main chemical in Epsom salts. When the students added the Epsom salts to the water, they were creating a magnesium sulfate solution. As the water was cools, the magnesium sulfate came out of the solution to form crystals once more.)

(Optional) STEAM Projects

Multi-chapter Activities

✂ **Periodic Table Project** – This chapter, the students will add the alkaline earth metals on SL p. 111 to their periodic table poster on SL p. 5.

Activities For This Chapter

✂ **Alkaline Earth Metals** – Several of the alkaline earth elements are responsible for giving fireworks their colors. Learn more about the chemistry of fireworks in the following video:

🖱 https://www.youtube.com/watch?v=nPHegSulI_M

✂ **Dissolving Calcium** – Have the students dissolve some calcium! You will need an egg, white vinegar, and a clear glass. Place the egg in the glass, and cover it with vinegar. Cover the glass, set it aside, and wait for 24 hours. The next day, pour out the vinegar, and observe the changes to the shell. (The shell of the egg contains calcium, which is dissolved by the acid in vinegar.)

✂ **Magnesium Veggies** – Have the students eat their veggies! Magnesium is one of the elements that is essential to keep our bodies working properly. We can get the magnesium we need from green veggies, but unfortunately when you boil veggies too long, much of the beneficial magnesium compounds come out. However, if you add a pinch of baking soda, the magnesium will stay put. This chapter, boil two batches of the green veggies of your choice: broccoli or spinach are good options. Add a pinch of baking soda to one of the pots, and have the students observe the difference.

Chapter 6: Grid Schedule

Supplies Needed

Demo	• White vinegar, Salt, 6 Pennies, Glass cup, 2 Iron nails
Projects	• 3 Balloons, Water, Ice

Chapter Summary

The chapter opens with the continuous miner breaking through the mine cavern's wall and into the Siberian lab of the Man With No Eyebrows. As it wreaks havoc in the lab, the miners on the other side are settling their differences and enjoying the last bit of the concert together. The twins zip off to their next location, Iceland! They appear on a huge tree stump in a forest and are mistaken for the foretold sun and moon. They quickly meet the members of the Kunningskapur—Ingrid the Hospitable, Magnus the Brave, and Harland the Wise. Harland the Wise serves as their local expert for their time in Iceland. They learn about transition metals and gold as the guild of three explains their quest for the three metals. The chapter ends with the main opponent of the Kunningskapur, Dagfinn the Wicked, crashing into the clearing!

Weekly Schedule

	Day 1	**Day 2**	**Day 3**	**Day 4**
Read	☐ Read the section entitled "Three Transition Metals" of Chapter 6 in *SSA Volume 7: Chemistry*.	☐ Read the section entitled "Fearless Gold" of Chapter 6 in *SSA Volume 7: Chemistry*.	☐ (*Optional*) Read one or all of the assigned pages from the encyclopedia of your choice.	☐ (*Optional*) Read one of the additional library books.
Write	☐ Fill out the Periodic Table Group Sheet on SL p. 33 on transition metals. ☐ Go over the vocabulary words and enter them into the Chemistry Glossary on SL p. 105.	☐ Fill out an Element Record Sheet on SL p. 34 on gold. ☐ (*Optional*) Work on the Iceland Map Sheet on SL p. 41.	☐ (*Optional*) Write narration on the Chemistry Notes Sheet on SL p. 39. ☐ Fill out the lab report sheet for the demonstration on SL p. 37.	☐ (*Optional*) Complete the copywork or dictation assignment and add it to the Chemistry Notes Sheet on SL p. 39. ☐ (*Optional*) Fill out the record sheet on SL p. 42 for one of the projects.
Do	☐ (*Optional*) Go on a Transition Metal Hunt.	☐ (*Optional*) Play with States of Matter.	☐ Do the demonstration entitled "Metal Plating."	☐ Work on the Periodic Table model.

Chapter 6: List Schedule

Chapter Summary

The chapter opens with the continuous miner breaking through the mine cavern's wall and into the Siberian lab of the Man With No Eyebrows. As it wreaks havoc in the lab, the miners on the other side are settling their differences and enjoying the last bit of the concert together. The twins zip off to their next location, Iceland! They appear on a huge tree stump in a forest and are mistaken for the foretold sun and moon. They quickly meet the members of the Kunningskapur—Ingrid the Hospitable, Magnus the Brave, and Harland the Wise. Harland the Wise serves as their local expert for their time in Iceland. They learn about transition metals and gold as the guild of three explains their quest for the three metals. The chapter ends with the main opponent of the Kunningskapur, Dagfinn the Wicked, crashing into the clearing!

Essential To-Do's

Read
- ☐ Read the section entitled "Three Transition Metals" of Chapter 6 in *SSA Volume 7: Chemistry*.
- ☐ Read the section entitled "Fearless Gold" of Chapter 6 in *SSA Volume 7: Chemistry*.

Write
- ☐ Fill out the Periodic Table Group Sheet on SL p. 33 on transition metals.
- ☐ Fill out an Element Record Sheet on SL p. 34 on gold.
- ☐ Fill out the lab report sheet for the demonstration on SL p. 37.
- ☐ Go over the vocabulary words and enter them into the Chemistry Glossary on SL p. 105.

Do
- ☐ Do the demonstration entitled "Metal Plating."
- ☐ Work on the Periodic Table model.

Optional Extras

Read
- ☐ Read one or all of the assigned pages from the encyclopedia of your choice.
- ☐ Read one of the additional library books.

Write
- ☐ Write a narration on the Chemistry Notes Sheet on SL p. 39.
- ☐ Complete the copywork or dictation assignment and add it to the Chemistry Notes Sheet on SL p. 39.
- ☐ Fill out the record sheet on SL p. 42 for one of the projects.
- ☐ Work on the Iceland Map Sheet on SL p. 41.

Do
- ☐ Go on a Transition Metal Hunt.
- ☐ Play with States of Matter.

Supplies Needed	
Demo	• White vinegar, Salt, 6 Pennies, Glass cup, 2 Iron nails
Projects	• 3 Balloons, Water, Ice

Chapter 6: Oh Iceland, Oh Iceland

Read: Gathering Information

Living Book Spine

- Chapter 6 of *The Sassafras Science Adventures Volume 7: Chemistry*

(Optional) Encyclopedia Readings

- *DK Eyewitness: The Elements* p. 22 (Transition Metal), p. 33 (Gold)
- *Scholastic's The Periodic Table* pp. 52-53 (Transition Metals), pp. 90-91 (Gold)
- *Usborne Science Encyclopedia* pp. 16-17 (Solids, liquids, and gases), pp. 30-31 (Metals)
- *Kingfisher Science Encyclopedia* pp. 156-157 (States of Matter), p. 183 (Metals)

(Optional) Additional Library Books

- *The Transition Elements: The 37 Transition Metals (Understanding the Elements of the Periodic Table)* by Mary-Lane Kamberg
- *Gold (The Elements)* by Sarah Angliss
- *Gold (True Books)* by Salvatore Tocci
- *What Is the World Made Of? All About Solids, Liquids, and Gases (Let's-Read-and-Find Out Science)* by Kathleen Weidner Zoehfeld and Paul Meisel
- *Solids, Liquids, and Gases (Rookie Read-About Science)* by Ginger Garrett

Write: Keeping a Notebook

SCIDAT Logbook Sheets

This chapter, you can have the students work on the map sheet. You can also have them fill out the record sheets for transition metals and gold along with adding to the notes sheet and glossary. The students should also complete a lab report sheet, and if they want, they can do a project record sheet. Here is the information they could include:

Iceland Map Sheet

This chapter, you can have the students look up the minerals found in Iceland. Here are a few possibilities:

- Calcite
- Sulfur

Here are two websites you can check out:

- https://www.whatson.is/icelandic-rocks-and-minerals/
- https://www.nationsencyclopedia.com/Europe/Iceland-MINING.html

Periodic Table Group Sheet - Transition Metals

ELEMENTS INCLUDED

- Scandium
- Titanium
- Vanadium
- Chromium
- Manganese
- Iron
- Cobalt
- Nickel
- Copper
- Zinc
- Yttrium
- Zirconium
- Niobium
- Molybdenum
- Technetium
- Ruthenium
- Rhodium
- Palladium
- Silver
- Cadmium
- Lutetium
- Hafnium
- Tantalum
- Tungsten
- Rhenium
- Osmium
- Iridium
- Platinum
- Gold
- Mercury

INTERESTING INFORMATION

- The transition metals are a group of elements found in the middle of the periodic table.
- For the most part, these elements are useful, hard, and shiny metals, such as iron, copper, gold, silver, and chromium.
- Some are catalysts, and some bond with other elements to form important compounds, such as alloys.
- The transition metals have high melting points.
- Many of these elements are excellent conductors of heat and electricity.
- Early jewelry was made from the transition metal copper.
- Some transition metals, such as platinum, iridium, and gold, are known as precious metals because they are rare or difficult to find, making these metals very valuable.
- Mercury is the only transition metal that is a liquid at room temperature.
- Transition metals are grey metals in their pure form with the notable exceptions of copper and gold. Even so, they form compounds that are quite colorful. In fact, some gemstones, fireworks, and even paints get their color from traces of transition metal compounds.

Element Record Sheet - Gold

GROUP NAME: Transition Metals

INFORMATION LEARNED

- Gold is very rare, making it a precious metal. Throughout history, gold has been associated with royalty and wealth.
- Gold is one of two transition metals that is not a grey metal. Instead, pure gold has a yellow hue.
- The symbol for gold is Au, which comes from the Latin word for gold, *"aurum."*
- The atomic number for gold is 79, and the atomic mass is 196.967.
- Gold is a soft metal, meaning that it can be easily polished and shaped into a number of different shapes.
- Gold is also desirable because it is resistant to corrosion, although it can be dissolved in some powerful acids. Because of this, gold is often found in pure form in nature.
- Gold can be found in flakes or nuggets lying on the ground or in the dirt. It can also be found in veins or as tiny particles in quartz rock underground.
- This metal is found in jewelry, electronic equipment, and crowns on teeth, and as money, in the

form of gold bullion, which is how banks store gold.
- Adding another transition metal, palladium, to gold lightens the color, turning it into white gold. Adding another transition metal, copper, to gold reddens the color, turning it into rose gold.
- The purity of gold is measured in carats – 24 carat gold is the purest. Alloys, or gold mixed with other elements, are usually 22, 18, 14, or 9 carats.

Chemistry Notes - States of Matter

The following is information that the students could add to their notes page:
- Elements and compounds can exist in three main states on Earth—solid, liquid, and gas. Solids have tightly packed molecules with fixed shape and volume. Liquids have widely spaced molecules with a fixed volume. Gases have independently moving molecules with no fixed shape or volume.
- There is also a fourth state of matter, called plasma. This state occurs when matter becomes an electrical-conducting medium—things like auroras, lightning, and welding arcs are all examples of plasma. Plasma can be created by heating gas to such a high temperature that it becomes ionized.

Vocabulary

Have the older students look up the following terms in the glossary in the appendix on pp. 133-134 or in a science encyclopedia. Then, have them copy each definition onto a blank index card or into their SCIDAT logbook.

- STATES OF MATTER – The different forms in which a substance can exist: solid, liquid, and gas.
- METAL – The largest class of elements, usually shiny and solid at room temperature.

(Optional) Copywork

Copywork Sentence

Transition metals are a group of elements in the middle of the periodic table.

Dictation Selection

The transition metals are a group of elements found in the middle of the periodic table. These elements are useful, hard, and shiny metals. The transition metals have high melting points. Many of these elements are excellent conductors of heat and electricity.

Do: Playing with Science

Scientific Demonstration: Metal Plating

Materials
- ☑ White vinegar
- ☑ Salt
- ☑ 6 Pennies
- ☑ Glass cup
- ☑ 2 Iron nails

Procedure

1. Have the students cover the bottom of the cup with a thin layer of salt.
2. Then, add the pennies, and cover them with the vinegar.
3. After 10 minutes, take the pennies out, and set them on a paper towel. Be sure to reserve the vinegar mixture.
4. Add one of the nails to the vinegar solution, and leave the other one next to the glass. Let both of them sit undisturbed for 45 minutes.
5. Take the nail out of the vinegar solution, and compare it to the nail that was left outside the glass.
6. Then, have the students draw what they see in the box on the lab report sheet on SL p. 37.

Explanation

The students should see that the iron nail from the vinegar solution has a thin, shiny, brownish coating on it. The coating may or may not be completely covering the nail. After the pennies were removed, the vinegar solution contained copper ions. Over time, they adhered to the iron nail, giving it a thin, shiny, brownish coating of copper. This is a small glimpse of how metal (copper) plating works.

Take It Further

While you are waiting, observe what is happening to the pennies. The students should see that over time the pennies develop a dull bluish tint after being removed from the vinegar solution. (When you first remove the pennies, they appear cleaner, but over time they developed a bluish tint. This color is the beginning of oxidation, the process that produces the dull green finish on copper.)

(Optional) STEAM Projects

Multi-chapter Activities

✂ PERIODIC TABLE PROJECT – This chapter, the students will add the transition metals on SL p. 111 to their periodic table poster on SL p. 5.

Activities For This Chapter

✂ TRANSITION METALS HUNT — Many of the elements in the transitional group are in items we have in our houses. Print a copy of the Transition Metal Hunt sheet from the appendix on p. 129. Then, let the students hunt around the house for the metals listed on the sheet and color in any of the elements they find. If you want to make a game out of this, the person with the most elements colored in wins.

✂ PLAYING WITH MATTER – Have the students play with the different states of matter. You will need three balloons, water, and ice. Fill one balloon with ice, one with water, and one with gas (air). Let the students explore each of the balloons and observe the differences. As they make their observations, ask them questions like these:

> ? Which one floats the best?
>
> ? Which one is easiest to control?
>
> ? Which one has the most interesting shape?

Chapter 7: Grid Schedule

\multicolumn{2}{c|}{Supplies Needed}	
Demo	• Steel wool, Vinegar, Jar with lid
Projects	• A tarnished silver item (jewelry or silverware), Tongs, Bowl, Aluminum foil, Baking soda, Hot water • Breakfast cereal, Strong magnet, Paper

Chapter Summary

The chapter opens with Magnus the Brave sprinting through the forest with the twins to save from Dagfinn the Wicked. He eventually sets the down and turns to face Dagfinn himself. Blaine, Tracey, Ingrid, and Harland quickly make their way to the village of Stin. They met an old man who believes Blaine and Tracey are the foretold sun and moon. The man shows them the way to the first treasure chest and the twins learn about zinc. Then, the man tells the group what they must do to find the next chest. Magnus rejoins them and the group heads up to the misty chasm to solve the riddle of the bridges. Blaine sees that Tracey has solved the riddle just as Dagfinn reappears. As Magnus and Dagfinn clash, Tracey asks the right question and one of the bridge keepers knock Dagfinn out. The group goes across the bridge and continues their quest. The chapter ends with the twins learning about iron as the group finds the second treasure chest.

Weekly Schedule

	Day 1	Day 2	Day 3	Day 4
Read	☐ Read the section entitled "Acquiring Zinc" of Chapter 7 in *SSA Volume 7: Chemistry*.	☐ Read the section entitled "Inquisitive Iron" of Chapter 7 in *SSA Volume 7: Chemistry*.	☐ (Optional) Read one or all of the assigned pages from the encyclopedia of your choice.	☐ (Optional) Read one of the additional library books.
Write	☐ Fill out an Element Record Sheet on SL p. 35 on zinc. ☐ Go over the vocabulary words and enter them into the Chemistry Glossary on SL p. 105.	☐ Fill out an Element Record Sheet on SL p. 36 on iron. ☐ (Optional) Work on the Iceland Map Sheet on SL p. 41.	☐ (Optional) Write narration on the Chemistry Notes Sheet on SL p. 40. ☐ Fill out the lab report sheet for the demonstration on SL p. 38.	☐ (Optional) Complete the copywork or dictation assignment and add it to the Chemistry Notes Sheet on SL p. 40. ☐ (Optional) Fill out the record sheet on SL p. 43 for one of the projects. ☐ (Optional) Take Chemistry Quiz #3.
Do	☐ (Optional) Do the More Redox activity.	☐ (Optional) Do the Magnetic Cereal activity.	☐ Do the demonstration entitled "Rusted."	☐ (Optional) Research and write a report about iron.

Chapter 7: List Schedule

Chapter Summary

The chapter opens with Magnus the Brave sprinting through the forest with the twins to save them from Dagfinn the Wicked. He eventually sets them down and turns to face Dagfinn himself. Blaine, Tracey, Ingrid, and Harland quickly make their way to the village of Stin. They meet an old man who believes Blaine and Tracey are the foretold sun and moon. The man shows them the way to the first treasure chest, and the twins learn about zinc. Then, the man tells the group what they must do to find the next chest. Magnus rejoins them, and the group heads up to the misty chasm to solve the riddle of the bridges. Blaine sees that Tracey has solved the riddle as Dagfinn reappears. As Magnus and Dagfinn clash, Tracey asks the right question, and one of the bridge keepers knocks Dagfinn out. The group goes across the bridge and continues their quest. The chapter ends with the twins learning about iron as the group finds the second treasure chest.

Essential To-Do's

Read
- ☐ Read the section entitled "Acquiring Zinc" of Chapter 7 in *SSA Volume 7: Chemistry*.
- ☐ Read the section entitled "Inquisitive Iron" of Chapter 7 in *SSA Volume 7: Chemistry*.

Write
- ☐ Fill out an Element Record Sheet on SL p. 35 on zinc.
- ☐ Fill out an Element Record Sheet on SL p. 36 on iron.
- ☐ Fill out the lab report sheet for the demonstration on SL p. 38.
- ☐ Go over the vocabulary words and enter them into the Chemistry Glossary on SL p. 105.

Do
- ☐ Do the demonstration entitled "Rusted."
- ☐ Work on the Periodic Table model.

Optional Extras

Read
- ☐ Read one or all of the assigned pages from the encyclopedia of your choice.
- ☐ Read one of the additional library books.

Write
- ☐ Write a narration on the Chemistry Notes Sheet on SL p. 40.
- ☐ Complete the copywork or dictation assignment and add it to the Chemistry Notes Sheet on SL p. 40.
- ☐ Fill out the record sheet on SL p. 43 for one of the projects.
- ☐ Work on the Iceland Map Sheet on SL p. 41.
- ☐ Take Chemistry Quiz #3.

Do
- ☐ Do the More Redox activity.
- ☐ Do the Magnetic Cereal activity.
- ☐ Research and write a report about iron.

Supplies Needed	
Demo	• Steel wool, Vinegar, Jar with lid
Projects	• A tarnished silver item (jewelry or silverware), Tongs, Bowl, Aluminum foil, Baking soda, Hot water • Breakfast cereal, Strong magnet, Paper

Chapter 7: The Three Metals Quest

Read: Gathering Information

Living Book Spine
📖 Chapter 7 of *The Sassafras Science Adventures Volume 7: Chemistry*

(Optional) Encyclopedia Readings
🔑 *DK Eyewitness: The Elements* p. 24 (Iron), p. 26 (Zinc)
🔑 *Scholastic's The Periodic Table* pp. 60-61 (Iron), p. 66 (Zinc)
🔑 *Usborne Science Encyclopedia* pp. 34-35 (Alloys), pp. 36-37 (Iron and Steel), pp. 80-81 (Oxidation and Reduction)
🔑 *Kingfisher Science Encyclopedia* p. 178 (Oxidation and Reduction), p. 198 (Iron), pp. 202-203 (Alloys)

(Optional) Additional Library Books
📖 *Zinc (True Books)* by Salvatore Tocci
📖 *Zinc (Elements)* by Leon Gray
📖 *Iron (Elements)* by Giles Sparrow
📖 *From Iron to Car (Start to Finish, Second Series)* by Shannon Zemlicka
📖 *The Story of Iron (First Book)* by Karen Fitzgerald

Write: Keeping a Notebook

SCIDAT Logbook Sheets

This chapter, you can have the students work on the map sheet. You can also have them fill out the record sheets for zinc and iron along with adding to the notes sheet and glossary. The students should also complete a lab report sheet, and if they want, they can do a project record sheet. Here is the information they could include:

Iceland Map Sheet

This chapter, you can have the students look up the industry found in Iceland. Here are a few possibilities:

- Aluminum Smelting
- Hydroelectric Power

Here are pages from the suggested atlas you can read:
📖 *DK Children's Illustrated Atlas* p. 54 (Northern Europe - section on Iceland)

Element Record Sheet - Zinc

Information Learned
- The symbol for zinc in Zn, the atomic number is 30, and the atomic mass is 65.39.

- Zinc is often found alongside of lead, and sometimes copper, gold, or silver, in sulfide ores.
- Zinc is a shiny transition metal that is known for its protective abilities.
- Zinc can be used to coat steel in a process called galvanizing. This stops water and oxygen from causing steel to rust.
- A compound of zinc is used in sunscreen to prevent harmful UV rays from damaging skin.
- Zinc is used in pyrotechnics to create a smoke effect.
- Zinc can easily mix with other metals, forming useful alloys, like brass.
- Zinc is also considered an essential element for many of the processes in the body.
- Zinc can also be mixed with carbon to make a battery that can power flashlights, toys, and other small electronics.

Element Record Sheet - Iron

Information Learned

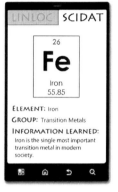

- Iron is probably the single most important transition metal to our modern society.
- The symbol for iron is Fe, which comes from the Latin word for iron, "*ferrum*." The atomic number for iron is 26, and the atomic mass is 55.85.
- Iron is mainly found in hematite and magnetite, which are quite abundant. In fact, about 90% of the metal that is refined is iron.
- Iron's crystal structure is strong, and when it is heated, the space between the grains shrinks further, making it even stronger.
- Iron mixed with carbon creates steel—the most important metal in the world. The resulting steel can be cast, formed, or welded into many different forms to create things like paper clips and the trussing, or framework, for skyscrapers.
- Iron working began more than 3,000 years ago when people learned how to separate iron by heating its ores with charcoal. As the technique was developed, iron replaced brass in tools and weapons.
- The core of the Earth is made from iron and nickel.
- The iron in our red blood cells makes it possible for these cells to carry oxygen, which makes this transition metal an essential element for life.
- Iron is one of the few transition metals that is ferromagnetic, meaning these elements have some magnetic properties on their own and can easily be used to create strong magnets.

Chemistry Notes - Oxidation and Reduction

The following is information that the students could add to their notes page:

- Oxidation and reduction reactions involve the movement of electrons in molecules and atoms. These two reactions always occur together and are known as redox reactions.
- An oxidation reaction happens when a molecule or an atom has a loss of electrons. A reduction reaction happens when a molecule or an atom has a gain of electrons.
- Combustion, photosynthesis, rusting, and respiration are all examples of redox reactions.

Vocabulary

Have the older students look up the following terms in the glossary in the appendix on pp. 133-134 or in a science encyclopedia. Then, have them copy each definition onto a blank index card or into their SCIDAT logbook.

- **ALLOY** – A mixture of two or more metals or a metal and a nonmetal.
- **REDOX REACTION** – A chemical reaction that involves the transfer of electrons.

(OPTIONAL) COPYWORK

Copywork Sentence

A redox reaction is one that involves the transfer of electrons.

Dictation Selection

Redox reactions involve two reactions that always occur together—oxidation and reduction. Both of these reactions involve the movement of electrons in molecules and atoms. An oxidation reaction happens when a molecule or an atom has a loss of electrons. A reduction reaction happens when a molecule or an atom has a gain of electrons. Combustion, photosynthesis, rusting, and respiration are all examples of redox reactions.

(OPTIONAL) QUIZ

This chapter, you can give the students a quiz based on what they learned in Chapters 6 and 7. You can find the quiz in the appendix on p. 147.

Quiz #3 Answers

1. D, B, C, A
2. Solid, liquid, gas
3. Bond
4. False (Gold is almost always found in its pure form in nature.)
5. Zinc
6. True
7. Electrons

DO: PLAYING WITH SCIENCE

SCIENTIFIC DEMONSTRATION: RUSTED

Materials
- ☑ Steel wool
- ☑ Vinegar
- ☑ Jar with lid

Procedure

1. Have the students place the steel wool in one of the jars and cover it with vinegar. Put the lid on the jar, and let the steel wool soak for 2 hours. (NOTE—This is done to remove any coating that may be on the steel wool so that the iron could react with the moist air.)
2. After 2 hours, have the students take the steel wool out, and set it on a the jar lid. Let it sit undisturbed for 30 minutes.
3. After a half an hour has passed, observe the changes in the steel wool. Have the students draw what they see in the box on the lab report sheet on SL p. 38.

Explanation

The students should see that the steel wool has turned a brownish-red color. This is because iron rusts, or oxidizes, when it is exposed to moist air. This is why iron we use in daily life is often coated with other metals or mixed with other elements to form rust-resistant alloys.

Take It Further

Have the students watch another redox reaction caused by air. You can do this by cutting an apple in half and letting it sit undisturbe for an hour. (When you check it after an hour, the students should see that the slices are brownish. This is due to a redox reaction between the apple flesh and the oxygen in the air.)

(Optional) STEAM Projects

Multi-chapter Activities

✂ PERIODIC TABLE PROJECT – This chapter, there is nothing to add to the periodic table.

Activities For This Chapter

✂ MORE REDOX - Have the students use a reduction reaction to clean a tarnished (oxidized) piece of silver. You will need a tarnished silver item (jewelry or silverware), tongs, a bowl, aluminum foil, baking soda, and hot water. Cover the bottom of the bowl with aluminum foil, and then sprinkle 1 tablespoon of baking soda over it. Add a cup of hot water, and mix until the baking soda is dissolved. Now, use the tongs to place the tarnished silver item into the solution. Wait a minute or two. (You will see bubbles form, and you might smell a rotten egg scent.) Then, use the tongs to take the item out and observe the changes. (The students should see that the item is much cleaner. This is because a redox reaction occurs between the aluminum, baking soda, and the tarnish, which is caused by a sulfur compound. This reaction removes the tarnish from the silver. Once the silver is exposed to the air again, sulfur in the air will cause another redox reaction, which produces the tarnish we see.)

✂ MAGNETIC CEREAL – Have the students see if their cereal is magnetic! You will need a breakfast cereal, a strong magnet, and a piece of paper. (**NOTE**—For the best results use an iron-fortified cereal, like cornflakes, and a neodymium magnet.) Have the students crush the cereal and put it on a piece of paper. Hold up the paper, and put the magent under the pile of cereal. Move the magnet around, and see if the cereal moves, too. If it does, your cereal has a lot of iron in it!

✂ IRON REPORT – Have the students research the uses of iron throughout history and write a one-paragraph report or create a poster advertisement about what they find.

Chapter 8: Grid Schedule

	Supplies Needed
Demo	• Neodymium magnets, Several types of objects (marbles, paper clips, paper, pins, plastic spoons, and more)
Projects	• Woolen mitten or glove. Fluorescent bulb • White glue, Water, Iron filings, Borax, Small neodymium magnets

Chapter Summary

The chapter opens with Blaine, Tracey, and the Kunningskapur find the final treasure chest, which they all hauled back to the village of Stin. The twins find a spot by themselves, enter the last of their SCIDAT data, and open up the LINLOC to find their next location—Japan! The twins land in a dojo in the middle of a karate class. The twins meet their local expert, Sensei Masaki, his student, Seth E. Prue, also known as the Hyper Goat, and Seth's friends, too. They participate in the class, learning about karate and lanthanides. They quickly learn that the dojo is being asked to rescue the CEO of the A.B.G. Nuclear Power Plant who has been taken by the Jaken. As they get ready for the rescue, the twins learn about neodymium. A plan is shared, and the group gets dressed in full blackout ninja uniforms. The chapter ends with the twins joining the group, becoming Neodymium Ninjas!

Weekly Schedule

	Day 1	Day 2	Day 3	Day 4
Read	☐ Read the section entitled "Kihuping Lanthanides" of Chapter 8 in *SSA Volume 7: Chemistry*.	☐ Read the section entitled "Neodymium Ninja Magnets" of Chapter 8 in *SSA Volume 7: Chemistry*.	☐ *(Optional)* Read one or all of the assigned pages from the encyclopedia of your choice.	☐ *(Optional)* Read one of the additional library books.
Write	☐ Fill out the Periodic Table Group Sheet on SL p. 44 on lanthanides. ☐ Go over the vocabulary word and enter it into the Chemistry Glossary on SL p. 106.	☐ Fill out an Element Record Sheet on SL p. 50 on neodymium. ☐ *(Optional)* Work on the Japan Map Sheet on SL p. 52.	☐ *(Optional)* Write narration on the Chemistry Notes Sheet on SL p. _. ☐ Fill out the lab report sheet for the demonstration on SL p. 48.	☐ *(Optional)* Complete the copywork or dictation assignment and add it to the Chemistry Notes Sheet on SL p. 50. ☐ *(Optional)* Fill out the record sheet on SL p. 53 for one of the projects.
Do	☐ *(Optional)* Do the Light-up Lanthanides activity.	☐ *(Optional)* Make Magnetic Slime.	☐ Do the demonstration entitled "Magnetic Exploration."	☐ Work on the Periodic Table model.

Chapter 8: List schedule

Chapter Summary

The chapter opens with Blaine, Tracey, and the Kunningskapur find the final treasure chest, which they all hauled back to the village of Stin. The twins find a spot by themselves, enter the last of their SCIDAT data, and open up the LINLOC to find their next location—Japan! The twins land in a dojo in the middle of a karate class. The twins meet their local expert, Sensei Masaki, his student, Seth E. Prue, also known as the Hyper Goat, and Seth's friends, too. They participate in the class, learning about karate and lanthanides. They quickly learn that the dojo is being asked to rescue the CEO of the A.B.G. Nuclear Power Plant who has been taken by the Jaken. As they get ready for the rescue, the twins learn about neodymium. A plan is shared, and the group gets dressed in full blackout ninja uniforms. The chapter ends with the twins joining the group, becoming Neodymium Ninjas!

Essential To-Do's

Read
- ☐ Read the section entitled "Kihuping Lanthanides" of Chapter 8 in *SSA Volume 7: Chemistry*.
- ☐ Read the section entitled "Neodymium Ninja Magnets" of Chapter 8 in *SSA Volume 7: Chemistry*.

Write
- ☐ Fill out the Periodic Table Group Sheet on SL p. 44 on lanthanides.
- ☐ Fill out an Element Record Sheet on SL p. 45 on neodymium.
- ☐ Fill out the lab report sheet for the demonstration on SL p. 48.
- ☐ Go over the vocabulary word and enter it into the Chemistry Glossary on SL p. 106.

Do
- ☐ Do the demonstration entitled "Magnetic Exploration."
- ☐ Work on the Periodic Table model.

Optional Extras

Read
- ☐ Read one or all of the assigned pages from the encyclopedia of your choice.
- ☐ Read one of the additional library books.

Write
- ☐ Write a narration on the Chemistry Notes Sheet on SL p. 50.
- ☐ Complete the copywork or dictation assignment and add it to the Chemistry Notes Sheet on SL p. 50.
- ☐ Fill out the record sheet on SL p. 53 for one of the projects.
- ☐ Work on the Japan Map Sheet on SL p. 52.

Do
- ☐ Do the Light-up Lanthanides activity.
- ☐ Make Magnetic Slime.

Supplies Needed	
Demo	• Neodymium magnets, Several types of objects (marbles, paper clips, paper, pins, plastic spoons, and more)
Projects	• Woolen mitten or glove. Fluorescent bulb • White glue, Water, Iron filings, Borax, Small neodymium magnets

Chapter 8: The Masaki-Do Dojo

Read: Gathering Information

Living Book Spine
- Chapter 8 of *The Sassafras Science Adventures Volume 7: Chemistry*

(Optional) Encyclopedia Readings
- *DK Eyewitness: The Elements* pp. 36-37 (Lanthanides)
- *Scholastic's The Periodic Table* pp. 128-129 (Lanthanoids), p. 131 (Neodymium)
- *Usborne Science Encyclopedia* pp. 232-235 (Magnetism)
- *Kingfisher Science Encyclopedia* pp. 342-343 (Magnets and Magnetism)

(Optional) Additional Library Books
- *The Lanthanides (Elements)* by Richard Beatty
- *What Makes a Magnet? (Let's-Read-and-Find-Out Science 2)* by Franklyn M. Branley and True Kelley
- *What Magnets Can Do (Rookie Read-About Science)* by Allan Fowler

Write: Keeping a Notebook

SCIDAT Logbook Sheets

This chapter, you can have the students work on the map sheet. You can also have them fill out the record sheets for lanthanides and neodymium along with adding to the notes sheet and glossary. The students should also complete a lab report sheet, and if they want, they can do a project record sheet. Here is the information they could include:

Japan Map Sheet

This chapter, you can have the students look up the minerals found in Japan. Here are a few possibilities:

- Iron ore
- Zinc
- Lead
- Copper
- Sulfur
- Gold
- Silver
- Tungsten
- Manganese

Here is a website you can check out:
- https://www.britannica.com/place/Japan/Resources-and-power

Periodic Table Group Sheet - Lanthanides

NOTE—Lanthanides are also known as lanthanoids or rare earth elements.

Elements Included
- Lanthanum
- Cerium
- Praseodymium

- Neodymium
- Pm-Promethium
- Samarium
- Europium
- Gadolinium
- Terbium
- Dysprosium
- Holmium
- Erbium
- Thulium
- Ytterbium

Interesting Information

- The lanthanides, or lanthanoids, are a group of 15 naturally occurring heavy, but soft metals.
- They are named after the first element in the group, lanthanum.
- These elements are called the rare earth metals, not because they are especially rare but the cause they were discovered later. They are typically found with other compounds, making them tricky to separate.
- In modern times, the lanthanide elements are used in touch screens and wind turbines as well as batteries for cell phones and hybrid cars.
- The lanthanide lutetium is found in space rocks.
- Several of the lanthanide elements have interesting magnetic properties. They are used to power the high-speed Maglev train. When samarium is mixed with cobalt, it creates a magnet that is 10,000 times more powerful than an iron magnet. Praseodymium can generate a magnetic field that cools things way down, so far down that scientists use it to recreate the coldest environments in the laboratory. Gadolinium is not magnetic at room temperature, but when you cool it to below freezing, its magnetic properties begin to appear.
- Europium and terbium are included in the ink of some currencies, such as the euro, because they glow under ultraviolet light. Europium glows red, and terbium glows green.

Element Record Sheet - Neodymium

Information Learned

- Neodymium is an important lanthanide element for our time.
- The symbol for neodymium is Nd. The atomic number is 60, and the atomic mass is 144.2.
- Neodymium comes from the Greek word *neos*, meaning "new," and *didymos*, meaning "twin." This is because when it was first discovered, it was part of what a scientist thought was an element considered the twin of lanthanum, so it was name didymium. More than 40 years later, didymium was found to actually be a combination of praseodymium and neodymium, hence, the name "New Twin."
- Neodymium is found in earbuds, computer hard drives, cell phones, and wind turbines. It is also used to create powerful magnets that help power trains and electric cars.
- As a permanent magnet, neodymium can pick up 1,000 times its weight.
- This element can help scientists determine the age of certain types of rocks or act as a catalyst in the chemical industry.
- Every day, neodymium is used in tanning booths and protective goggles as well holding dentures together.
- In its pure form, it oxidizes quickly in the air, so pure neodymium is either coated or stored in oil.

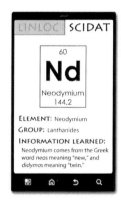

Chemistry Notes - Magnetism

The following is information that the students could add to their notes page:

- Magnetism is an invisible force that attracts different kinds of metals, especially iron and steel.

Materials that put out this force are described as magnetic.
- Magnets typically have a north and south pole.
- If you have two magnets, the north pole of one magnet will be attracted to the south pole of the other magnet because unlike poles attract each other, whereas like poles repel each other.

VOCABULARY

Have the older students look up the following term in the glossary in the appendix on pp. 133-134 or in a science encyclopedia. Then, have them copy the definition onto a blank index card or into their SCIDAT logbook.

 MAGNET – An object that attracts iron, steel, and metals.

(OPTIONAL) COPYWORK

Copywork Sentence

Lanthanides are also called rare earth metals.

Dictation Selection

Magnetism is an invisible force that attracts different kinds of metals, especially iron and steel. Materials that put out this force are described as magnetic. Several of the lanthanide elements have magnetic properties, including neodymium.

DO: PLAYING WITH SCIENCE

SCIENTIFIC DEMONSTRATION: MAGNETIC EXPLORATION

Materials
- ☑ Neodymium magnets (If you cannot get neodymium magnets, you can use bar or horseshoe magnets.)
- ☑ Several types of objects (marbles, paper clips, paper, pins, plastic spoons, and more)

Procedure
1. Allow the students to play with the magnets and the objects. Let them see how they are attracted to each other or how they repel each other.
2. Then, have the students try to pick up the objects with the magnets.
3. Have them record these testing materials (objects), along with if they were attracted to the magnet, on the lab report sheet on SL p. 48.

Explanation

The students should see that the magnets attracted some objects but not others. The objects that magnets attract typically have iron or steel in them. Magnets also attract other magnets as long as their poles are opposite. North attracts south, and south attracts north. If the two poles are the same, they will repel, or push each other away.

Take It Further

Have the students make a magnetic pendulum using the principles they learned in the demonstration. You can see an example of this at the following website:

 https://teachbesideme.com/magnet-pendulum/

(Optional) STEAM Projects

Multi-chapter Activities

✂ **Periodic Table Project** – This chapter, the students will add the lanthanides on SL p. 111 to their periodic table poster on SL p. 5.

Activities For This Chapter

✂ **Light-up Lanthanides** – Terbium, a lanthanide, is often used to coat fluorescent bulbs. This is because it glows when it is hit by a beam of electrons. Have the students excite some electrons and make a bulb glow without plugging it in. You will need a woolen mitten or glove and a fluorescent bulb. Head into a dark room, rub the bulb with the woolen mitten, and watch what happens! (When you rub the bulb, you create static electricity, which is basically excited electrons!)

✂ **Magnetic Slime** – Have the students make and play with magnetic slime. You will need white glue, water, iron filings, some Borax, and several small neodymium magnets. In a plastic baggie, mix 4 oz white glue, 4 oz of water, and about a half teaspoon of iron filings. In a cup, mix a quarter cup of water and half a teaspoon of Borax. Then, add the Borax solution to the baggie, and massage the bag for a few minutes until a nice firm slime has formed. Then the magnetic fun begins! Have the students use the magnets to play around with the slime and pull it in different directions. They can also test the strength of a magnet by seeing how much of the slime it can pull up.

Chapter 9: Grid Schedule

	Supplies Needed
Demo	• Bite-sized food, such as raisins or cereal puffs or M&M's, Timer
Projects	• A working smoke detector, Bottle of baby powder • Computer with Internet access

Chapter Summary
The chapter opens with the Masaki-do Neodymium Ninjas on their way to the nuclear power plant to rescue the CEO, something all other groups of ninjas haven't been able to do. On the way, they learn about nuclear energy and actinides. We switch to Paul Sims, who is forming a plan to stay out of jail, one that includes his old schoolmate, Cecil Sassafras. Back with the ninjas, we see them secretly entering the power plant via the water intake. It's a tense moment, but the group makes it in, whereas other groups have failed. The group makes its way through the power plant, encountering the Jaken, and a fight ensues. In the fight, Seth is lost, but the group has to keep going. The Jaken continue to pursue and fight with them, but the Masaki-do make it to the CEO's office, where they find Hayato Doi and Natsuki Saito. The chapter ends with the twins learning about uranium in an explosive way.

Weekly Schedule

	Day 1	Day 2	Day 3	Day 4
Read	☐ Read the section entitled "Actinide Bailout" of Chapter 9 in *SSA Volume 7: Chemistry*.	☐ Read the section entitled "Trapping Uranium" of Chapter 9 in *SSA Volume 7: Chemistry*.	☐ *(Optional)* Read one or all of the assigned pages from the encyclopedia of your choice.	☐ *(Optional)* Read one of the additional library books.
Write	☐ Fill out the Periodic Table Group Sheet on SL p. 46 on actinides. ☐ Go over the vocabulary word and enter it into the Chemistry Glossary on SL p. 106.	☐ Fill out an Element Record Sheet on SL p. 47 on uranium. ☐ *(Optional)* Work on the Japan Map Sheet on SL p. 52.	☐ *(Optional)* Write narration on the Chemistry Notes Sheet on SL p. 51. ☐ Fill out the lab report sheet for the demonstration on SL p. 49.	☐ *(Optional)* Complete the copywork or dictation assignment and add it to the Chemistry Notes Sheet on SL p. 51. ☐ *(Optional)* Fill out the record sheet on SL p. 47 for one of the projects. ☐ *(Optional)* Take Chemistry Quiz #4.
Do	☐ *(Optional)* Do the Detecting Smoke activity.	☐ *(Optional)* Play with the Nuclear Neighborhood.	☐ Do the demonstration entitled "Radioactive Decay."	☐ Work on the Periodic Table model.

Chapter 9: List Schedule

Chapter Summary

The chapter opens with the Masaki-do Neodymium Ninjas on their way to the nuclear power plant to rescue the CEO, something all other groups of ninjas haven't been able to do. On the way, they learn about nuclear energy and actinides. We switch to Paul Sims, who is forming a plan to stay out of jail, one that includes his old schoolmate, Cecil Sassafras. Back with the ninjas, we see them secretly entering the power plant via the water intake. It's a tense moment, but the group makes it in, whereas other groups have failed. The group makes its way through the power plant, encountering the Jaken, and a fight ensues. In the fight, Seth is lost, but the group has to keep going. The Jaken continue to pursue and fight with them, but the Masaki-do make it to the CEO's office, where they find Hayato Doi and Natsuki Saito. The chapter ends with the twins learning about uranium in an explosive way.

Essential To-Do's

Read
- ☐ Read the section entitled "Actinide Bailout" of Chapter 9 in *SSA Volume 7: Chemistry*.
- ☐ Read the section entitled "Trapping Uranium" of Chapter 9 in *SSA Volume 7: Chemistry*.

Write
- ☐ Fill out the Periodic Table Group Sheet on SL p. 46 on actinides.
- ☐ Fill out an Element Record Sheet on SL p. 47 on uranium.
- ☐ Fill out the lab report sheet for the demonstration on SL p. 49.
- ☐ Go over the vocabulary word and enter it into the Chemistry Glossary on SL p. 106_.

Do
- ☐ Do the demonstration entitled "Radioactive Decay."
- ☐ Work on the Periodic Table model.

Optional Extras

Read
- ☐ Read one or all of the assigned pages from the encyclopedia of your choice.
- ☐ Read one of the additional library books.

Write
- ☐ Write a narration on the Chemistry Notes Sheet on SL p. 51.
- ☐ Complete the copywork or dictation assignment and add it to the Chemistry Notes Sheet on SL p. 51.
- ☐ Fill out the record sheet on SL p. 54 for one of the projects.
- ☐ Work on the Japan Map Sheet on SL p. 52.
- ☐ Take Chemistry Quiz #4.

Do
- ☐ Do the Detecting Smoke activity.
- ☐ Play with the Nuclear Neighborhood.

Supplies Needed	
Demo	• Bite-sized food, such as raisins or cereal puffs or M&M's, Timer
Projects	• A working smoke detector, Bottle of baby powder • Computer with Internet access

Chapter 9: The Nuclear Rescue Mission

Read: Gathering Information

Living Book Spine
- Chapter 9 of *The Sassafras Science Adventures Volume 7: Chemistry*

(Optional) Encyclopedia Readings
- *DK Eyewitness: The Elements* pp. 40-41 (Actinides), p. 42 (Uranium)
- *Scholastic's The Periodic Table* pp. 140-141 (Actinoids), pp. 144-145 (Uranium)
- *Usborne Science Encyclopedia* pp. 114-115 (Radioactivity), pp. 116-117 (Nuclear Power)
- *Kingfisher Science Encyclopedia* pp. 348-349 (Power Plants)

(Optional) Additional Library Books
- *Radioactive Elements* by Tom Jackson
- *The 15 Lanthanides and the 15 Actinides (Understanding the Elements of the Periodic Table)* by Kristi Lew
- *Nuclear Energy: Amazing Atoms (Powering Our World)* by Amy S. Hansen
- *Nuclear Energy (Discovery Channel School Science)* by Michael Burgan and Nancy Cohen

Write: Keeping a Notebook

SCIDAT Logbook Sheets

This chapter, you can have the students work on the map sheet. You can also have them fill out the record sheets for actinides and uranium along with adding to the notes sheet and glossary. The students should also complete a lab report sheet, and if they want, they can do a project record sheet. Here is the information they could include:

Japan Map Sheet

This chapter, you can have the students look up the industry found in Japan. Here are a few possibilities:

- Electronics
- Nuclear power

Here are pages from the suggested atlas you can read:
- *DK Children's Illustrated Atlas* pp. 102-103 (Japan)

Periodic Table Group Sheet - Actinides

NOTE—Actinides are also known as actinoids or radioactive rare earth elements.

Elements Included
- Actinium
- Thorium
- Protactinium

- Uranium
- Neptunium
- Plutonium
- Americium
- Curium
- Berkelium
- Californium
- Einsteinium
- Fermium
- Mendelevium
- Nobelium

Interesting Information

- The actinides, or actinoids, are a group of 15 heavy metals. They were also named for the first element in the group actinium, which is so radioactive that it gives off a blue glow in the dark.
- Only two of the actinides occur naturally in large quantities—uranium and thorium.
- The rest of the actinides are created in the lab, are present in minute quantities in nature, or make an appearance in nuclear reactors and particle accelerators.
- Many for the actinides are radioactive, which means that they easily break apart, releasing energy and potentially damaging particles. This is because their nuclei are heavy, with 89-plus protons in them.
- With the exception of uranium and thorium, all of these elements were discovered within the last century or so.
- Even though many of these elements are dangerously radioactive, they are used by astronauts, doctors, and firefighters. Curium is used to provide power on space missions. Americium is used in smoke detectors and portable X-ray machines. Plutonium was once used to power pacemakers; now it is used in the nuclear industry. Actinium is used in neutron soil probes. And thorium is used in making parts for aircrafts and spacecrafts.

Element Record Sheet - Uranium

Information Learned

- Uranium is the actinide that is key to nuclear energy, but it is a powerful, heavy, and poisonous element.
- The symbol for uranium is U. The atomic number for uranium is 92, and the atomic mass is 238.0.
- If you fire a neutron at an uranium atom, the nucleus splits to form uranium-235 as it releases a ton of energy. This releases several more neutrons that impact with several more uranium atoms, setting off a chain reaction. This chain reaction can be slowed down and controlled to produce nuclear energy, or it can be uncontrolled, which results in a bomb that can flatten cities.
- In a nuclear power plant, enriched uranium is splits into two small nuclei and uranium-235, releasing a ton of energy. This energy heats up water, producing steam. The steam rises and is used to turn turbines, which generate electrical energy. The steam then condenses and is recycled.
- Depleted uranium, which is left over from the uranium-enriching process, has been used as ships ballast, bullets, and tank armor.

Chemistry Notes - Nuclear Energy

The following is information that the students could add to their notes page:

- Within the nucleus of an atom, there is a large amount of nuclear energy.
- Some atoms with a large number of protons and neutrons present in the nucleus are considered unstable. This means that these atoms are more likely to release some of the nuclear energy from

the nucleus as a particle, making the atom radioactive.
- The atom can emit three types of radiation:
  1. Alpha particles, which consist of two protons and two neutrons.
  2. Beta particles, which are extremely high-energy electrons.
  3. Gamma particles, which are high-energy electromagnetic waves.

Vocabulary

Have the older students look up the following term in the glossary in the appendix on pp. 133-134 or in a science encyclopedia. Then, have them copy the definition onto a blank index card or into their SCIDAT logbook.

- RADIOACTIVE DECAY – The process by which a nucleus ejects particles through radiation, becoming the nucleus of a series of different elements until stability is reached.

(Optional) Copywork

Copywork Sentence

Many of the actinide elements are radioactive.

Dictation Selection

The nucleus of an atom contains a large amount of energy known as nuclear energy. This makes some atoms with a large number of protons and neutrons in the nucleus unstable. These atoms are more likely to release some of the nuclear energy from its nucleus as a particle, making the atom radioactive.

(Optional) Quiz

This chapter, you can give the students a quiz based on what they learned in chapters 8 and 9. You can find the quiz in the appendix on p. 149.

Quiz #4 Answers
1. B, A
2. False (For magnets, like poles repel each other, while unlike poles attract each other.)
3. True
4. Very
5. False (Many of the elements in the actinide group are radioactive.)
6. Generating power
7. Alpha, gamma, beta

Do: Playing with Science

Scientific Demonstration: Radioactive Decay

Materials
- ☑ Bite-sized food, such as raisins, cereal puffs, or M&Ms
- ☑ Timer

Procedure
1. Give the students 32 pieces of the bite-sized food.

2. After 2 minutes, have them eat 16 pieces.
3. After 2 more minutes, have them eat 8 pieces.
4. After 2 more minutes, have them eat 4 pieces.
5. After 2 more minutes, have them eat 2 pieces.
6. After 2 more minutes, have them eat 1 piece.
7. After 2 more minutes, have them break the 1 piece in half and eat one of the halves.
8. After 2 more minutes, have the students eat any of the remaining crumbs.
9. Have the students complete the lab report sheet on SL p. 49.

Explanation

This demonstration was meant to give a students a mental picture of how a half-life works. Many of the actinide elements are radioactive, which means that they are unstable, so the elements decay with a half life. The half-life period depends upon the element and how radioactive it is.

Take It Further

Have the students learn more about nuclear power by watching the following video:

https://www.youtube.com/watch?v=d7LO8lL4Ai4

NOTE—This video does touch on the dangers of nuclear power versus other power methods. Please preview this video to make sure it is appropriate for your child.

(Optional) STEAM Projects

Multi-chapter Activities

✂ PERIODIC TABLE PROJECT – This chapter, the students will add the actinides on SL p. 111 to their periodic table poster on SL p. 5.

Activities For This Chapter

✂ DETECTING SMOKE – Many modern smoke detectors use americium to detect smoke. To have the students learn about how this works, you will need a working smoke detector and a bottle of baby powder. Have the students hold the detector above the bottle of baby power and squeeze the bottle gently to create a few puffs of baby powder. (This time the students should see that the smoke detector goes off. This is because the americium in the smoke detector charges the nearby air, and when new molecules float through this zone, it changes the charge and causes the alarm to sound.)

✂ NUCLEAR NEIGHBORHOOD – Have the students play with the EPA's Radtown USA website:

https://www.epa.gov/radtown/explore-sources-radiation-neighborhood

Chapter 10: Grid Schedule

	Supplies Needed
Demo	• Alum powder, Ammonia, Clear jar, Water
Projects	• No additional supplies needed

Chapter Summary

The chapter opens with Seth E. Prue making a stunning reentry, saving the day. With the nuclear power plant in safe hands, the twins zip off to their next location—Singapore! They land in a news van, where they see an interview with Aishaanya, their local expert. They learn about main group metals and the Merlion Fashion Show. When the twins are discovered, they are interviewed by Sadie, THE DROP news anchor, before she chases after Aishaanya. Blaine and Tracy follow the reporters. In the craziness, they are picked out by Aishaanya, and they leave the area with her and her bodyguard, Brutus. On the way to her building, she says that Tracey will be her new model and Blaine will be Brutus's new apprentice. Once at the headquarters for Aishaanya, they meet Bisaam, a designer and artist. He is putting the finishing touches on a periodic table made out of cans! The twins admire his work and learn about aluminum from Aishaanya. The chapter ends with the destructive entrance of Tamina Threads, a colleague-turned-competitor.

Weekly Schedule

	Day 1	**Day 2**	**Day 3**	**Day 4**
Read	☐ Read the section entitled "Modeling Main Group Metals" of Chapter 10 in *SSA Volume 7: Chemistry*.	☐ Read the section entitled "Bisaam's Aluminum Cans" of Chapter 10 in *SSA Volume 7: Chemistry*.	☐ *(Optional)* Read one or all of the assigned pages from the encyclopedia of your choice.	☐ *(Optional)* Read one of the additional library books.
Write	☐ Fill out the Periodic Table Group Sheet on SL p. 55 on main group metals. ☐ Go over the vocabulary word and enter it into the Chemistry Glossary on SL p. 106.	☐ Fill out an Element Record Sheet on SL p. 56 on aluminum. ☐ *(Optional)* Work on the Singapore Map Sheet on SL p. 63.	☐ *(Optional)* Write narration on the Chemistry Notes Sheet on SL p. 61. ☐ Fill out the lab report sheet for the demonstration on SL p. 59.	☐ *(Optional)* Complete the copywork or dictation assignment and add it to the Chemistry Notes Sheet on SL p. 61. ☐ *(Optional)* Fill out the record sheet on SL p. 64 for one of the projects.
Do	☐ *(Optional)* Do the Indium Ink Research.	☐ *(Optional)* Watch the Aluminum Foil Reaction.	☐ Do the demonstration entitled "Aluminum Gel."	☐ Work on the Periodic Table model.

Chapter 10: List schedule

Chapter Summary

The chapter opens with Seth E. Prue making a stunning reentry, saving the day. With the nuclear power plant in safe hands, the twins zip off to their next location—Singapore! They land in a news van, where they see an interview with Aishaanya, their local expert. They learn about main group metals and the Merlion Fashion Show. When the twins are discovered, they are interviewed by Sadie, THE DROP news anchor, before she chases after Aishaanya. Blaine and Tracy follow the reporters. In the craziness, they are picked out by Aishaanya, and they leave the area with her and her bodyguard, Brutus. On the way to her building, she says that Tracey will be her new model and Blaine will be Brutus's new apprentice. Once at the headquarters for Aishaanya, they meet Bisaam, a designer and artist. He is putting the finishing touches on a periodic table made out of cans! The twins admire his work and learn about aluminum from Aishaanya. The chapter ends with the destructive entrance of Tamina Threads, a colleague-turned-competitor.

Essential To-Do's

Read
- ☐ Read the section entitled "Modeling Main Group Metals" of Chapter 10 in *SSA Volume 7: Chemistry*.
- ☐ Read the section entitled "Bisaam's Aluminum Cans" of Chapter 10 in *SSA Volume 7: Chemistry*.

Write
- ☐ Fill out the Periodic Table Group Sheet on SL p. 55 on main group metals.
- ☐ Fill out an Element Record Sheet on SL p. 56 on aluminum.
- ☐ Fill out the lab report sheet for the demonstration on SL p. 59.
- ☐ Go over the vocabulary word and enter it into the Chemistry Glossary on SL p. 106.

Do
- ☐ Do the demonstration entitled "Aluminum Gel."
- ☐ Work on the Periodic Table model.

Optional Extras

Read
- ☐ Read one or all of the assigned pages from the encyclopedia of your choice.
- ☐ Read one of the additional library books.

Write
- ☐ Write a narration on the Chemistry Notes Sheet on SL p. 61.
- ☐ Complete the copywork or dictation assignment and add it to the Chemistry Notes Sheet on SL p. 61.
- ☐ Fill out the record sheet on SL p. 64 for one of the projects.
- ☐ Work on the Singapore Map Sheet on SL p. 63.

Do
- ☐ Do the Indium Ink Research.
- ☐ Watch the Aluminum Foil Reaction.

Supplies Needed	
Demo	• Alum powder, Ammonia, Clear jar, Water
Projects	• No additional supplies needed

Chapter 10: Singapore's Merlion Fashion Extravaganza

Read: Gathering Information

Living Book Spine

- Chapter 10 of *The Sassafras Science Adventures Volume 7: Chemistry*

NOTE—On the right-hand side the periodic table, things begin to divert a bit. Some resources will group the elements according to the element at the top of the column, that is, Boron Group, Oxygen Group, and so on—*DK Eyewitness: The Elements* groups the elements in this way. Other resources will group the elements according to similar properties, that is, Metalloids, Nonmetals, and so on—*Scholastic's The Periodic Table* groups the elements this way. Although both methods are technically correct, in *The Sassafras Science Adventures Volume 7: Chemistry*, we have chosen to go with the second, more common method of grouping the elements based on similar characteristics. Here is an article about why these differences occur:

- https://elementalscience.com/blogs/news/the-periodic-table

(Optional) Encyclopedia Readings

- *DK Eyewitness: The Elements* p. 46 (Aluminum), pp. 48-49 (part 2 of Boron Elements), p 53 (Lead)
- *Scholastic's The Periodic Table* pp. 102-103 (Poor Metals), pp. 104-105 (Aluminum), pp. 106-111 (Remaining Poor Metals)
- *Usborne Science Encyclopedia* p. 33 (Poor Metals)
- *Kingfisher Science Encyclopedia* p. 200 (Aluminum)

(Optional) Additional Library Books

- *The Boron Elements: Boron, Aluminum, Gallium, Indium, Thallium (Understanding the Elements of the Periodic Table)* by Heather Hasan
- *Aluminum* by Heather Hasan
- *Lead (Understanding the Elements of the Periodic Table)* by Kristi Lew

Write: Keeping a Notebook

SCIDAT Logbook Sheets

This chapter, you can have the students work on the map sheet. You can also have them fill out the record sheets for main group metals and aluminum along with adding to the notes sheet and glossary. The students should also complete a lab report sheet, and if they want, they can do a project record sheet. Here is the information they could include:

Singapore Map Sheet

This chapter, you can have the students look up the minerals found in Singapore. Here are a few possibilities:

- Silver
- Gold

Here is a website you can check out:

🖱 https://www.mapsofworld.com/singapore/singapore-mineral-map.html

Periodic Table Group Sheet - Main Group Metals

ELEMENTS INCLUDED

- Aluminum
- Gallium
- Indium
- Thallium
- Tin
- Lead
- Bismuth

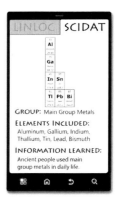

INTERESTING INFORMATION

- Main group metals include elements from group 13 (aluminum, gallium, indium, and thallium), group 14 (tin and lead), and group 15 (bismuth).
- These metals are also known as ordinary metals, base metals, or poor metals.
- These metals are post-transition, meaning they come after the block of transition metals on the periodic table.
- They are called "poor" metals because they are typically softer than other metals with low melting and boiling points. However, these metals are still relatively strong.
- These metals can conduct electricity and heat well. They are also easy to shape.
- Ancient Egyptians used the main group metal, lead, as eyeliner in hopes that it would protect them against illness. Ancient Romans lined their pipes with lead, and the first printing press had lead in it. Nowadays we know that lead is poisonous to humans.

Element Record Sheet - Aluminum

INFORMATION LEARNED

- Aluminum is a silver-gray metal used in building many of the machines that power our modern age.
- The symbol for aluminum is Al. The atomic number for aluminum is 13, and the atomic mass is 26.98.
- Aluminum is the third-most abundant element on Earth, but it is difficult to get because it is tightly bound in the mineral ore, bauxite. Because it takes so much energy to isolate aluminum, there is a high demand for recycled aluminum. Recycling aluminum takes 95% less energy to produce than removing the element from bauxite.
- Aluminum was once considered a noble metal, like silver and gold. Napoleon III had a whole set of cutlery, including plates, made that he reserved for his most important guests.
- Aluminum is relatively light for a metal, but it is also strong.
- It is used to make airplanes, circuit boards, cans, and foil.
- Aluminum oxide, a compound with aluminum, is the main component of both rubies and sapphires.

Chemistry Notes - Periodic Table

The following is information that the students could add to their notes page:

- The periodic table can have several different visual representations. One periodic table will be full of color, dividing elements into families, or categories, with names. One periodic table will have different blocks of elements in different colors. And yet another periodic table will have columns, or groups, in different colors.
- The periodic table is a way for us to visually show the relationships between the elements. Like human relationships, these elemental relationships can be defined, or shown, in different ways.
- Plus, as technology grows, our ability to define those relationships grows more clearly as well. And as we experiment with the elements, we discover new things that help to shape the periodic table. So, although a newer periodic table may depict new elements, we have created and a deeper understanding of the relationships between elements—it doesn't make an older version wrong. It's just a different snapshot of our understanding of the elements.

VOCABULARY

Have the older students look up the following term in the glossary in the appendix on pp. 133-134 or in a science encyclopedia. Then, have them copy the definition onto a blank index card or into their SCIDAT logbook.

- POOR METAL – A group of metals that are soft and weak.

(OPTIONAL) COPYWORK

Copywork Sentence

Main group metals are also known as poor metals.

Dictation Selection

Main group metals include elements from group 13, group 14, and group 15 of the periodic table. These metals come after the block of transition metals on the periodic table. They are called "poor" metals because they are typically softer than other metals with low melting and boiling points. However, these metals are still relatively strong.

DO: PLAYING WITH SCIENCE

SCIENTIFIC DEMONSTRATION: ALUMINUM GEL

Materials
- ☑ Alum powder
- ☑ Ammonia
- ☑ Clear jar
- ☑ Water

Procedure
1. Have the students add half cup of water to the jar.
2. Then, have them add a teaspoon of alum powder and stir until the powder dissolves.
3. Next, pour in a quarter cup of ammonia.
4. Allow the jar to sit undisturbed for about 5 minutes.

5. Finally, have the students draw what they see in the box on the lab report sheet on SL p. 49.

Explanation

The students should see the solution turn cloudy as soon as the ammonia is added. Then after a few minutes, a white gel will form at the bottom of the jar. This gel is a compound of a main group metal, aluminum hydroxide. (NOTE—This reaction has similar properties to the one the students did for Chapter 5. Both reactions involve the formation of a precipitate.)

Take It Further

Have the students examine another aluminum-containing compound found in your kitchen, aluminum foil. Have them examine a sheet and note its appearance. If you want to learn about how foil is made, you can watch the following video:

https://www.youtube.com/watch?v=f4OTj9yNOak

(Optional) STEAM Projects

Multi-chapter Activities

- **Periodic Table Project** – This chapter, the students will add the main group metals on SL p. 111 to their periodic table poster on SL p. 5.

Activities For This Chapter

- **Indium Ink Research** - Have the students learn about indium, which is used to make an electrically conductive ink. This ink is used in UPC codes, solar cells, and LCD screens. (NOTE—Older students can share what they have learned as a poster or in a paragraph.)

- **Aluminum Foil** – Have the students observe a neat reaction in which aluminum foil gets dissolved. The video can be viewed at the following link:

  https://www.youtube.com/watch?v=AAKdc7PO3J0

Chapter 11: Grid Schedule

Supplies Needed	
Demo	• Silly Putty™ or other silicone polymer, Baggie, Ice, Bowl, Hot water
Projects	• Gel glue, Water, Borax powder • Magic sand

Chapter Summary

The chapter opens with Tracey getting ready for the fashion show as she learns about metalloids from Aishaanya. The perspective then shifts back and forth from Blaine and Brutus to Tracey and Aishaanya. We see Blaine track down the missing fashion line. They break into Tamina's warehouse, expecting to find the garments there, but all they find is Tamina. So, the two return to Aishaanya, Inc. We see Tracey getting a glimpse at the new periodic table fashion line she will be wearing that has been designed by Rosemary and Bisaam. The clothing is beautifully woven in different metals and metalloids. Tracey learns more about the metalloid silicone, which is a major part of the dress she will wear. Then, we shift to the Man With No Eyebrows who has returned to North Pecan Street, defeated. The chapter ends with Blaine and Tracey reunited and everyone ready for the fashion show to begin!

Weekly Schedule

	Day 1	**Day 2**	**Day 3**	**Day 4**
Read	☐ Read the section entitled "Observing Metals" of Chapter 11 in *SSA Volume 7: Chemistry*.	☐ Read the section entitled "Silicone Trends" of Chapter 11 in *SSA Volume 7: Chemistry*.	☐ *(Optional)* Read one or all of the assigned pages from the encyclopedia of your choice.	☐ *(Optional)* Read one of the additional library books.
Write	☐ Fill out the Periodic Table Group Sheet on SL p. 57 on metalloids. ☐ Go over the vocabulary words and enter them into the Chemistry Glossary on SL pp. 106-107.	☐ Fill out an Element Record Sheet on SL p. 58 on silicone. ☐ *(Optional)* Work on the Singapore Map Sheet on SL p. 63.	☐ *(Optional)* Write narration on the Chemistry Notes Sheet on SL p. 61. ☐ Fill out the lab report sheet for the demonstration on SL p. 64.	☐ *(Optional)* Complete the copywork or dictation assignment and add it to the Chemistry Notes Sheet on SL p. 61. ☐ *(Optional)* Fill out the record sheet on SL p. 64 for one of the projects. ☐ *(Optional)* Take Chemistry Quiz #5.
Do	☐ *(Optional)* Make some Boron Slime.	☐ *(Optional)* Play with Magic Sand.	☐ Do the demonstration entitled "Silicone Putty."	☐ Work on the Periodic Table model.

Chapter 11: List Schedule

Chapter Summary

The chapter opens with Tracey getting ready for the fashion show as she learns about metalloids from Aishaanya. The perspective then shifts back and forth from Blaine and Brutus to Tracey and Aishaanya. We see Blaine track down the missing fashion line. They break into Tamina's warehouse, expecting to find the garments there, but all they find is Tamina. So, the two return to Aishaanya, Inc. We see Tracey getting a glimpse at the new periodic table fashion line she will be wearing that has been designed by Rosemary and Bisaam. The clothing is beautifully woven in different metals and metalloids. Tracey learns more about the metalloid silicone, which is a major part of the dress she will wear. Then, we shift to the Man With No Eyebrows who has returned to North Pecan Street, defeated. The chapter ends with Blaine and Tracey reunited and everyone ready for the fashion show to begin!

Essential To-Do's

Read
- ☐ Read the section entitled "Observing Metals" of Chapter 11 in *SSA Volume 7: Chemistry*.
- ☐ Read the section entitled "Silicone Trends" of Chapter 11 in *SSA Volume 7: Chemistry*.

Write
- ☐ Fill out the Periodic Table Group Sheet on SL p. 57 on metalloids.
- ☐ Fill out an Element Record Sheet on SL p. 58 on silicone.
- ☐ Fill out the lab report sheet for the demonstration on SL p. 60.
- ☐ Go over the vocabulary words and enter them into the Chemistry Glossary on SL pp. 106-107.

Do
- ☐ Do the demonstration entitled "Silicone Putty."
- ☐ Work on the Periodic Table model.

Optional Extras

Read
- ☐ Read one or all of the assigned pages from the encyclopedia of your choice.
- ☐ Read one of the additional library books.

Write
- ☐ Write a narration on the Chemistry Notes Sheet on SL p. 61.
- ☐ Complete the copywork or dictation assignment and add it to the Chemistry Notes Sheet on SL p. 61.
- ☐ Fill out the record sheet on SL p. 64 for one of the projects.
- ☐ Work on the Singapore Map Sheet on SL p. 63.
- ☐ Take Chemistry Quiz #5.

Do
- ☐ Make some Boron Slime.
- ☐ Play with Magic Sand.

	Supplies Needed
Demo	• Silly Putty™ or other silicone polymer, Baggie, Ice, Bowl, Hot water
Projects	• Gel glue, Water, Borax powder • Magic sand

Chapter 11: Models and Mysteries

Read: Gathering Information

Living Book Spine

📖 Chapter 11 of *The Sassafras Science Adventures Volume 7: Chemistry*

(Optional) Encyclopedia Readings

🔑 *DK Eyewitness: The Elements* p. 47 (Boron), p. 51 (Silicon), p. 52 (Germanium), pp. 56-57 (Arsenic and Antimony)

🔑 *Scholastic's The Periodic Table* pp. 116-117 (Metalloids), p. 119 (Silicon), pp. 118, 120-125 (Remaining Metalloids)

🔑 *Usborne Science Encyclopedia* pp. 238-239 (Digital Electronics)

🔑 *Kingfisher Science Encyclopedia* pp. 360-361 (Conductors)

(Optional) Additional Library Books

📖 *The Carbon Elements: Carbon, Silicon, Germanium, Tin, Lead (Understanding the Elements of the Periodic Table)* by Brian Belval

📖 *The Invention of the Silicon Chip: A Revolution in Daily Life* by Windsor Chorlton

Write: Keeping a Notebook

SCIDAT Logbook Sheets

This chapter, you can have the students work on the map sheet. You can also have them fill out the record sheets for atoms and elements along with adding to the notes sheet and glossary. The students should also complete a lab report sheet, and if they want, they can do a project record sheet. Here is the information they could include:

Singapore Map Sheet

This chapter, you can have the students look up the industry found in Singapore. However, this country is small, and the main industry there is finance, so you may not find anything. You can read the following pages about Southeast Asia:

📖 *DK Children's Illustrated Atlas* pp. 104-105 (Southeast Asia)

Periodic Table Group Sheet - Metalloids

Elements Included

- Boron
- Silicon
- Germanium
- Arsenic
- Antimony
- Tellurium
- Polonium

Interesting Information
- Metalloids include the elements from group 13 (boron), group 14 (silicon and germanium), group 15 (arsenic and antimony), and group 16 (tellurium and polonium).
- These elements are also known as semi-metals or semiconductors.
- They look like metals and even have some metallic properties.
- Metalloids are often brittle and don't like to behave like metals typically do.
- Ancient Chinese would put boron in the glaze on their roof tiles as well as in pottery and porcelain. A compound of boron, borax, was one of the items exported from Tibet and traded along the Silk Road.
- Arsenic is a deadly chemical that can be found in apple seeds.

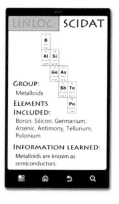

Element Record Sheet - Silicon
Information Learned
- Silicon is one of the elements that has made the digital age possible.
- The symbol for silicon is Si. The atomic number for silicon is 14, and the atomic mass is 28.09.
- Silicon has some of the properties of a metal, but it is a glassy, off-white lump in pure form. It is typically found in nature bound to other elements because it doesn't like to be on its own.
- When combined with boron and phosphorus, silicon is the semiconductor that gave rise to the Computer Age through the silicon chip.
- Silicon is the second-most abundant element on Earth. It is found in sand, quartz, and many other minerals.
- It can also be used in lubricants, adhesives, and clocks.
- Silicon was in the boots that Neil Armstrong wore as he first set foot on the moon. These silicon rubber boots protected the astronauts from the extremely high and low temperatures in space.

Chemistry Notes - Conductivity
The following is information that the students could add to their notes page:
- Conductivity is the ability of a material to conduct, or pass along, electricity or heat.
- Typically, metals are great conductors, whereas nonmetals are not.
- Semiconductors, like silicon and germanium, fall somewhere in between these.

Vocabulary
Have the older students look up the following terms in the glossary in the appendix on pp. 133-134 or in a science encyclopedia. Then, have them copy each definition onto a blank index card or into their SCIDAT logbook.

- ♪ METALLOID – An element that shares some of the properties of metals and nonmetals.
- ♪ SEMICONDUCTOR – A type of material that acts as a conductor or as an insulator depending on its temperature.

(Optional) Copywork
Copywork Sentence
Metalloids are also known as semi-metals or semiconductors.

Dictation Selection

Metalloids include the elements from group 13, group 14, group 15, and group 16. These elements are also known as semi-metals or semiconductors. Metalloids look like metals and even have some metallic properties.

(Optional) Quiz

This chapter, you can give the students a quiz based on what they learned in Chapters 10 and 11. You can find the quiz in the appendix on p. 151.

Quiz #5 Answers
1. C,B,A
2. Relationships
3. Students' answers can include the following: get hot easily, electricity flows easily through them, shiny, strong, versatile
4. True
5. Students' answers can include the following: semiconductors, similar to metals, often brittle
6. An abundant
7. Conductivity

Do: Playing with Science

Scientific Demonstration: Silicone Putty

Materials
- ☑ Silly Putty™ or other silicone polymer
- ☑ Baggie
- ☑ Ice
- ☑ Bowl
- ☑ Hot water

Procedure
1. Have the students observe and play with the putty. They can pull it out slowly and quickly to see the differences in how the putty reacts. They can roll it into a ball and flatten it into a disc to see if it feels different.
2. Then, place the putty in the baggie and seal it. Fill the bowl with ice and nestle the baggie into the ice. Wait for 5 minutes.
3. Have the students pull the putty out of the baggie and observe if it is cool to the touch. Have them quickly repeat the activities with the putty that were done in step 1. Ask the students:

   ? Does the putty act differently after it has been in the ice?

4. Next, place the putty back in the baggie, and seal it once more. Dump the ice out of the bowl and let it come to room temperature. After it does, fill the bowl halfway with hot water, and nestle the baggie into the water. You may need to weigh the baggie down with a glass or a rock. Wait for 5 minutes.
5. Have the students pull the putty out of the baggie and observe if it is warm to the touch. Have them quickly repeat the activities with the putty that were done in step 1. Ask the students the following:

   ? Does the putty act differently after it has been in the hot water?

6. Then, have the students fill out the lab report sheet on SL p. 58.

Explanation

The students should see that the putty stretches much farther when pulled slowly, and they should see that it does bounce when it is rolled in a ball. Silly putty is a silicone polymer with long chains of silicon, oxygen, carbon, and hydrogen. When you pull on it slowly, the chains have time to line up, and it can stretch further. When the putty is chilled, there is less energy in the substance, and the chains take much longer to line up. So the chilled putty is won't pull as far and won't bounce as well. When the putty is heated, there is more energy in the substance, and the chains can line up more quickly. So the warmed putty is will pull farther and bounce higher than the room-temperature putty.

Take It Further

Have the students look for another silicon compound—quartz! Quartz is a silicon dioxide compound that is often found in rocks. Head outside and look for quartz rocks in your area. Then identify and observe the types of quartz you find. (You can share with your students that the different colors of quartz come from other elements. Smoky quartz is brown thanks to aluminum. Rose quartz is pink thanks to a bit of titanium and manganese. And amethyst, a purple quartz, gets its color from a bit of iron.)

(Optional) STEAM Projects

Multi-chapter Activities

- **Periodic Table Project** – This chapter, the students will add the metalloids on SL p. 111 to their periodic table poster on SL p. 5.

Activities For This Chapter

- **Boron Slime** – Have the students make slime using borax, a boron-containing compound. You will need gel glue, water, and Borax, which can be found in the laundry aisle. In a plastic baggie, have the students mix equal parts of glue and water. Meanwhile, in a cup, mix a quarter cup of water with half a teaspoon of Borax. Then, add the Borax solution to the baggie, and have the students massage the bag for a few minutes until a nice, firm slime has formed.

- **Magic Sand** – Have the students play with magic sand, which is silicon dioxide (sand) coated with a polymer that makes it stay dry in water. Here are a few ideas to explore the properties of magic sand, along with more of the science behind it:
    - https://www.stevespanglerscience.com/lab/experiments/magic-hydrophobic-sand/

Chapter 12: Grid Schedule

	Supplies Needed
Demo	• Can of dark cola soda, Glass, Dirty pennies
Projects	• Limestone or chalk, Cup, White vinegar

Chapter Summary

The chapter opens at the Merlion Fashion Extravaganza with Tracey walking down the runway in the Chameleon dress. The show is a success for Aishaanya, Inc. and Blaine and Tracey enter the data they learned, preparing to zip off to their next location in Great Britain. Back at Uncle Cecil's we learn of his basement dinner preparations before he hears someone at the trap door. Meanwhile, the twins have landed in a small dome, and they quickly learn that they will be playing the Carboxynitro Games. The host of the show, the Unseen One, tells them about nonmetals and the biodome that they will be competing in. The twins learn that they will be competing against other twin groups in a crazy Garden-of-Eden version of an obstacle course with a zip-lining twist. They learn about carbon and what will happen if they don't follow the course rules—they will get flushed! The chapter ends with the twins beginning the course and following the rules, but not everyone does. Two of the teams get immediately flushed!

Weekly Schedule

	Day 1	**Day 2**	**Day 3**	**Day 4**
Read	☐ Read the section entitled "Menacing Nonmetals" of Chapter 12 in *SSA Volume 7: Chemistry*.	☐ Read the section entitled "Bubbles of Carbon" of Chapter 12 in *SSA Volume 7: Chemistry*.	☐ *(Optional)* Read one or all of the assigned pages from the encyclopedia of your choice.	☐ *(Optional)* Read one of the additional library books.
Write	☐ Fill out the Periodic Table Group Sheet on SL p. 66 on nonmetals. ☐ Go over the vocabulary word and enter it into the Chemistry Glossary on SL p. 107.	☐ Fill out an Element Record Sheet on SL p. 67 on carbon. ☐ *(Optional)* Work on the Great Britain Map Sheet on SL p. 72.	☐ *(Optional)* Write narration on the Chemistry Notes Sheet on SL p. 73. ☐ Fill out the lab report sheet for the demonstration on SL p. 70.	☐ *(Optional)* Complete the copywork or dictation assignment and add it to the Chemistry Notes Sheet on SL p. 73. ☐ *(Optional)* Fill out the record sheet on SL p. 75 for one of the projects.
Do	☐ *(Optional)* Do the Smelly Sulfur activity.	☐ *(Optional)* Test for Carbon Rocks.	☐ Do the demonstration entitled "Shiny Pennies."	☐ Work on the Periodic Table model.

Chapter 12: List schedule

Chapter Summary

The chapter opens at the Merlion Fashion Extravaganza with Tracey walking down the runway in the Chameleon dress. The show is a success for Aishaanya, Inc. and Blaine and Tracey enter the data they learned, preparing to zip off to their next location in Great Britain. Back at Uncle Cecil's we learn of his basement dinner preparations before he hears someone at the trap door. Meanwhile, the twins have landed in a small dome, and they quickly learn that they will be playing the Carboxynitro Games. The host of the show, the Unseen One, tells them about nonmetals and the biodome that they will be competing in. The twins learn that they will be competing against other twin groups in a crazy Garden-of-Eden version of an obstacle course with a zip-lining twist. They learn about carbon and what will happen if they don't follow the course rules—they will get flushed! The chapter ends with the twins beginning the course and following the rules, but not everyone does. Two of the teams get immediately flushed!

Essential To-Do's

Read
- ☐ Read the section entitled "Menacing Nonmetals" of Chapter 12 in *SSA Volume 7: Chemistry*.
- ☐ Read the section entitled "Bubbles of Carbon" of Chapter 12 in *SSA Volume 7: Chemistry*.

Write
- ☐ Fill out the Periodic Table Group Sheet on SL p. 66 on nonmetals.
- ☐ Fill out an Element Record Sheet on SL p. 67 on carbon.
- ☐ Fill out the lab report sheet for the demonstration on SL p. 70.
- ☐ Go over the vocabulary word and enter it into the Chemistry Glossary on SL p. 107.

Do
- ☐ Do the demonstration entitled "Shiny Pennies."
- ☐ Work on the Periodic Table model.

Optional Extras

Read
- ☐ Read one or all of the assigned pages from the encyclopedia of your choice.
- ☐ Read one of the additional library books.

Write
- ☐ Write a narration on the Chemistry Notes Sheet on SL p. 73.
- ☐ Complete the copywork or dictation assignment and add it to the Chemistry Notes Sheet on SL p. 73.
- ☐ Fill out the record sheet on SL p. 75 for one of the projects.
- ☐ Work on the Great Britain Map Sheet on SL p. 72.

Do
- ☐ Do the Smelly Sulfur activity.
- ☐ Test for Carbon Rocks.

Supplies Needed	
Demo	• Can of dark cola soda, Glass, Dirty pennies
Projects	• Limestone or chalk, Cup, White vinegar

Chapter 12: Britain's Carboxynitro Games

READ: Gathering Information

LIVING BOOK SPINE

📖 Chapter 12 of *The Sassafras Science Adventures Volume 7: Chemistry*

(OPTIONAL) ENCYCLOPEDIA READINGS

- *DK Eyewitness: The Elements* p. 50 (Carbon)
- *Scholastic's The Periodic Table* pp. 160-161 (Nonmetals), pp. 162-163 (Carbon)
- *Usborne Science Encyclopedia* pp. 50-53 (Carbon)
- *Kingfisher Science Encyclopedia* p. 170 (Carbon), pp. 174-175 (Organic Chemistry)

(OPTIONAL) ADDITIONAL LIBRARY BOOKS

📖 *Nonmetals (Material Matters/Freestyle Express)* by Carol Baldwin
📖 *Carbon* by Linda Saucerman
📖 *Carbon (True Books: Elements)* by Salvatore Tocci
📖 *Phosphorus (Elements)* by Richard Beatty
📖 *Sulfur (The Elements)* by Richard Beatty

WRITE: Keeping a Notebook

SCIDAT LOGBOOK SHEETS

This chapter, you can have the students work on the map sheet. You can also have them fill out the record sheets for nonmetals and carbon along with adding to the notes sheet and glossary. The students should also complete a lab report sheet, and if they want, they can do a project record sheet. Here is the information they could include:

Great Britain Map Sheet

This chapter, you can have the students look up the minerals found in Great Britain. Here are a few possibilities:

- Chalk
- Limestone
- Silver
- Tungsten
- Tin
- Gold

Here are two websites you can check out:

🖱 https://www.azomining.com/Article.aspx?ArticleID=94
🖱 https://www.mapsofworld.com/united-kingdom/united-kingdom-mineral-map.html

Periodic Table Group Sheet - Nonmetals

ELEMENTS INCLUDED

- Carbon
- Nitrogen
- Oxygen
- Phosphorus
- Sulfur
- Selenium

Interesting Information
- Nonmetals include elements from group 14 (carbon), group 15 (nitrogen and phosphorus), and group 16 (oxygen, sulfur, and selenium).
- These elements are not metals, and so they lack the strength that metals provide. However, five of them are essential to life, and the other one (selenium) is needed in trace amounts for human life.
- The nonmetal elements can be gases, liquids, or solids, and they behave differently in chemistry. They all have significantly lower melting points and are poor conductors of heat and electricity.
- Nonmetals are far more common on Earth than metals are.
- In ancient Greece, they burned the nonmetal sulfur to get ride of pests. New York City also did the same in the late 1800s to prevent the spread of diseases. Pure sulfur is bright yellow, and it is a key ingredient in gunpowder. Sulfur is found oozing out of active volcanoes, but sulfur is also found in proteins and enzymes in our bodies.
- White phosphorus burns readily in air, and phosphorus can be poisonous. However, this nonmetal is part of our DNA and an essential part of our bones and teeth.
- Selenium is used to color glass red and is in photoelectric cells. It is also found in nature and needed by humans for our metabolism and thyroid, although too much of it would poison us.

Element Record Sheet - Carbon
Information Learned
- Carbon is referred to as the king of the elements because it is found in millions of different compounds, many of which are important to life as we know it.
- The symbol for carbon is C. The atomic number for carbon is 6, and the atomic mass is 12.01.
- Carbon is a nonmetal that can be found in charcoal, diamonds, graphite, and other different forms.
- It is the fourth-most abundant element in the universe.
- Carbon can bond in several different ways, meaning that it can form many different shapes and sizes of molecules. Because of the versatility, it is a part of almost all living matter. It is the primary component of fats, proteins, carbohydrates, and nucleic acids, like DNA.
- There are more than 9 million different compounds of carbon that we know about.
- The carbon cycle shows how this element moves through the environment on Earth. It is released by humans in exhalation and waste. This carbon is absorbed by plants and then eaten by animals to begin the cycle again.

Chemistry Notes - Organic Chemistry
The following is information that the students could add to their notes page:
- Organic chemistry is part of chemistry that looks at the science behind carbon compounds. It's often referred to as the chemistry of life because so many carbon compounds are essential to life as we know it.
- When this branch of chemistry was originally founded, it dealt only with compounds made by living organisms, but as technology has grown, so has organic chemistry.
- Now, it includes the compounds of life plus man-made compounds, such as plastics and other industrial products.

Vocabulary

Have the older students look up the following term in the glossary in the appendix on pp. 133-134 or in a science encyclopedia. Then, have them copy each definition onto a blank index card or into their SCIDAT logbook.

↻ **Nonmetal** – A class of elements that can be non-shiny solids or gases.

(Optional) Copywork

Copywork Sentence

Nonmetals can be gases, liquids, or solids.

Dictation Selection

Nonmetals include elements from group 14, group 15, and group 16. These elements can be gases, liquids, or solids, and they behave differently in chemistry. They all have significantly lower melting points and are poor conductors of heat and electricity. Nonmetals are far more common on Earth than metals are.

Do: Playing with Science

Scientific Demonstration: Shiny Pennies

Materials
- ☑ Can of dark cola soda
- ☑ Glass
- ☑ Dirty pennies

Procedure
1. Have the students place several dirty pennies in a cup. Have them draw or take a picture of the penny in the box on the lab report sheet on SL p. 70.
2. Then, pour enough cola into the cup to cover the pennies, set the cup aside, and let it sit undisturbed overnight.
3. The next morning, fish out the pennies, and have the students observe the differences. Have the students draw or glue a picture of the penny in the box on the lab report sheet.
4. When they are done, pour the cola down the drain. (**Note**—Do not drink the cola because it now has copper ions in it!)

Explanation

The students should see that the pennies are much cleaner after sitting overnight in the cola. This is because dark cola has phosphoric acid in it, something that gives the soda its tangy flavor. This acid also breaks up the copper-oxygen compound that, with time, makes pennies dark and dull.

Take It Further

Have the students see if they can get the same results from other kitchen acids, like lemon juice, tea, milk, and other types of soda.

(Optional) STEAM Projects

Multi-chapter Activities

- ✂ PERIODIC TABLE PROJECT – This chapter, the students will add nonmetals on SL p. 111 to their periodic table poster on SL p. 5.

Activities For This Chapter

- ✂ SMELLY SULFUR – Have the students experience the smell of sulfur! You will need a vegetable with a high sulfur content, such as cabbage, brussel sprouts, or turnips. Cut the vegetable in half, smell both halves, and set one half aside. Then, cut the remaining half in half again, and boil the two quarters. After 10 minutes remove one of the quarters, and have the students compare the smells between the cooked and uncooked portions. Wait 10 more minutes, and then remove the remaining quarter from the boiling water. Have the students compare the smells of all three slices. (The students should note an increasing "rotten-eggs" smell in the cooked portions of the vegetable. The heat causes the bonds to break, which releases the stinky, sulfur-containing compound, hydrogen sulfide.)

- ✂ CARBON ROCKS – Have the students test for the presence of limestone. Have them place a piece of limestone or chalk in a cup, and pour white vinegar over it. Have the students observe what happens. (The students should see bubbles forming on the chalk or rock.)

Chapter 13: Grid Schedule

	Supplies Needed
Demo	• Yeast, Water, Cup, Empty water bottle, Hydrogen peroxide, Food coloring, Liquid dish soap
Projects	• Candle, Match, Glass jar

Chapter Summary

The chapter opens with the arrival of Paul Sims in Uncle Cecil's basement. Apparently, he's come to reconnect with his old middle-school pals, Summer and Cecil. Back in the Carboxynitro Games, Blaine and Tracey are making real progress through the obstacle course's winding path. They've been climbing and digging, all while following the rules about connecting with the guidelines. As they make their way through, they run into some of the other twin teams, some of whom are kind, some of whom are not. Back at Uncle Cecil's, we find out that Paul Sims has managed to get invited to stay the night. Meanwhile, back in the Biodome, Blaine and Tracey learn about oxygen and nitrogen from the Unseen One as they work through more obstacles. They end up being one of four sets of twins who are left in the game. The chapter ends with one of the most difficult obstacles yet, one that will test their need for oxygen.

Weekly Schedule

	Day 1	Day 2	Day 3	Day 4
Read	☐ Read the section entitled "Never Mind, Oxygen" of Chapter 13 in *SSA Volume 7: Chemistry*.	☐ Read the section entitled "Iced-over Nitrogen" of Chapter 13 in *SSA Volume 7: Chemistry*.	☐ (*Optional*) Read one or all of the assigned pages from the encyclopedia of your choice.	☐ (*Optional*) Read one of the additional library books.
Write	☐ Fill out an Element Record Sheet on SL p. 68 on oxygen. ☐ Go over the vocabulary word and enter it into the Chemistry Glossary on SL p. 107.	☐ Fill out an Element Record Sheet on SL p. 69 on nitrogen. ☐ (*Optional*) Work on the Great Britain Map Sheet on SL p. 72.	☐ (*Optional*) Write narration on the Chemistry Notes Sheet on SL p. 74. ☐ Fill out the lab report sheet for the demonstration on SL p. 71.	☐ (*Optional*) Complete the copywork or dictation assignment and add it to the Chemistry Notes Sheet on SL p. 74. ☐ (*Optional*) Fill out the record sheet on SL p. 76 for one of the projects. ☐ (*Optional*) Take Chemistry Quiz #6.
Do	☐ (*Optional*) Do the Breathing Flame activity.	☐ (*Optional*) Learn about the Nitrogen Cycle.	☐ Do the demonstration entitled "Oxygen Overflow."	

Chapter 13: List Schedule

Chapter Summary

The chapter opens with the arrival of Paul Sims in Uncle Cecil's basement. Apparently, he's come to reconnect with his old middle-school pals, Summer and Cecil. Back in the Carboxynitro Games, Blaine and Tracey are making real progress through the obstacle course's winding path. They've been climbing and digging, all while following the rules about connecting with the guidelines. As they make their way through, they run into some of the other twin teams, some of whom are kind, some of whom are not. Back at Uncle Cecil's, we find out that Paul Sims has managed to get invited to stay the night. Meanwhile, back in the Biodome, Blaine and Tracey learn about oxygen and nitrogen from the Unseen One as they work through more obstacles. They end up being one of four sets of twins who are left in the game. The chapter ends with one of the most difficult obstacles yet, one that will test their need for oxygen.

Essential To-Do's

Read

☐ Read the section entitled "Never Mind, Oxygen" of Chapter 13 in *SSA Volume 7: Chemistry*.

☐ Read the section entitled "Iced-over Nitrogen" of Chapter 13 in *SSA Volume 7: Chemistry*.

Write

☐ Fill out an Element Record Sheet on SL p. 68 on oxygen.

☐ Fill out an Element Record Sheet on SL p. 69 on nitrogen.

☐ Fill out the lab report sheet for the demonstration on SL p. 71.

☐ Go over the vocabulary word and enter it into the Chemistry Glossary on SL p. 107.

Do

☐ Do the demonstration entitled "Oxygen Overflow."

Optional Extras

Read

☐ Read one or all of the assigned pages from the encyclopedia of your choice.

☐ Read one of the additional library books.

Write

☐ Write a narration on the Chemistry Notes Sheet on SL p. 74.

☐ Complete the copywork or dictation assignment and add it to the Chemistry Notes Sheet on SL p. 74.

☐ Fill out the record sheet on SL p. 76 for one of the projects.

☐ Work on the Great Britain Map Sheet on SL p. 72.

☐ Take Chemistry Quiz #6.

Do

☐ Do the Breathing Flame activity.

☐ Learn about the Nitrogen Cycle.

Supplies Needed	
Demo	• Yeast, Water, Cup, Empty water bottle, Hydrogen peroxide, Food coloring, Liquid dish soap
Projects	• Candle, Match, Glass jar

Chapter 13: The Three Challenges

Read: Gathering Information

Living Book Spine

📖 Chapter 13 of *The Sassafras Science Adventures Volume 7: Chemistry*

(Optional) Encyclopedia Readings

🔖 *DK Eyewitness: The Elements* pp. 54-55 (The Nitrogen Group), pp. 58-59 (The Oxygen Group)
🔖 *Scholastic's The Periodic Table* pp. 168-177 (Remaining Nonmetals)
🔖 *Usborne Science Encyclopedia* pp. 92-93 (Organic Chemistry)
🔖 *Kingfisher Science Encyclopedia* p. 171 (Nitrogen and Oxygen)

(Optional) Additional Library Books

📖 *The Nitrogen Elements (Understanding the Elements of the Periodic Table)* by Greg Roza
📖 *The Oxygen Elements: Oxygen, Sulfur, Selenium, Tellurium, Polonium (Understanding the Elements of the Periodic Table)* by Laura La Bella
📖 *Nitrogen (True Books: Elements)* by Salvatore Tocci
📖 *Oxygen (True Books: Elements)* by Salvatore Tocci

Write: Keeping a Notebook

SCIDAT Logbook Sheets

This chapter, you can have the students work on the map sheet. You can also have them fill out the record sheets for oxygen and nitrogen along with adding to the notes sheet and glossary. The students should also complete a lab report sheet, and if they want, they can do a project record sheet. Here is the information they could include:

Great Britain Map Sheet

This chapter, you can have the students look up the industry found in Great Britain. Here are a few possibilities:

- Gas
- Oil

Here are pages from the suggested atlas you can read:

📖 *DK Children's Illustrated Atlas* pp. 56-57 (British Isles)

Element Record Sheet - Oxygen

Information Learned

- The symbol for oxygen is O. The atomic number for oxygen is 8, and the atomic mass is 16.00.

- Oxygen is the third-most abundant element in the universe and the most abundant element in the Earth's crust.
- Oxygen is a colorless and odorless gas, but it is the driving force behind many reactions known as oxidation reactions. This type of reaction is what causes iron to rust and wood, plus other types of fuel, to burn. It's the presence of oxygen that gives rocket fuel the power to burn with enough force to launch the rocket.
- It readily combines with other elements to release energy.
- Oxygen is necessary to life because our cells use it as fuel for the chemical reactions in our bodies. Animals need oxygen to survive. They release a carbon dioxide, which plants need to survive. The plants use the carbon dioxide as fuel and release oxygen, which animals use. In this way, oxygen cycles around our planet.
- This nonmetal is also found high in the atmosphere as ozone, which protects us from harmful ultraviolet rays.

Element Record Sheet - Nitrogen

Information Learned

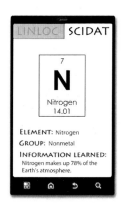

- Nitrogen makes up 78% of the Earth's atmosphere, and the human body is 3% of this element.
- The symbol for nitrogen is N. The atomic number for nitrogen is 7, and the atomic mass is 14.01.
- This element was discovered in 1771 by Daniel Rutherford, who called it "noxious air."
- Nitrogen is a fairly unreactive gas that is essential to life on Earth due to the strong bond between two nitrogen atoms. However, when this bond is broken, it releases a tremendous amount of energy, so nitrogen is often used in explosives.
- Nitrogen compounds, along with phosphorus compounds, are used in fertilizers because without these elements, plants would wither and die.
- Liquid nitrogen is very, very cold and will freeze just about anything that comes into contact with it.
- Nitrogen compounds are also used in plastics, textiles, and dyes, as well as in coolants for computers and semiconductors.
- The nitrogen cycle explains how nitrogen from the air and soil is absorbed by bacteria and changed into a usable format for plants. These plants are eaten by animals and humans. When they die, the nitrogen compounds are returned to the soil and air to begin the cycle again.

Chemistry Notes - Elements for Life

The following is information that the students could add to their notes page:

- There are six elements that are common to all life and thus considered essential. These are carbon, hydrogen, nitrogen, oxygen, phosphorus, and sulfur. You can use the acronym CHNOPS to remember these.
- Carbon is considered the backbone of life, whereas oxygen is considered the fuel.
- Humans also have the following elements present in their bodies: calcium, potassium, sodium, chlorine, and magnesium.
- We also have a need for other trace elements like fluorine for strong teeth, zinc for enzyme action,

selenium for metabolism, and iron in the blood to help transport oxygen.

Vocabulary

Have the older students look up the following term in the glossary in the appendix on pp. 133-134 or in a science encyclopedia. Then, have them copy each definition onto a blank index card or into their SCIDAT logbook.

- **Essential Element** – An element that is essential to life on Earth, such as carbon, hydrogen, nitrogen, or oxygen.

(Optional) Copywork

Copywork Sentence

Oxygen, nitrogen, and carbon are all nonmetals that are essential to life.

Dictation Selection

There are six elements that are common to all life and thus considered essential. These are carbon, hydrogen, nitrogen, oxygen, phosphorus, and sulfur. Carbon is considered the backbone of life, whereas oxygen is considered the fuel.

(Optional) Quiz

This chapter, you can give the students a quiz based on what they learned in Chapters 12 and 13. You can find the quiz in the appendix on p. 153.

Quiz #6 Answers

1. A,B
2. Students' answers can include the following: some are gases, not like metals, life on Earth is based on these elements
3. False (Pencil lead and diamonds both contain carbon.)
4. 80%
5. True
6. Carbon, Hydrogen, Nitrogen, Oxygen, Phosphorus, Sulfur
7. Carbon

Do: Playing with Science

Scientific Demonstration: Oxygen Overflow

Materials
- ☑ Yeast
- ☑ Water
- ☑ Cup
- ☑ Empty water bottle
- ☑ Hydrogen peroxide
- ☑ Food coloring
- ☑ Liquid dish soap

Procedure

1. In the cup, have the students mix together a packet (2 tsp) of yeast with a quarter cup of warm water and set aside.
2. In the bottle, have the students mix half a cup of hydrogen peroxide, 3 to 5 drops of food coloring, and 7 to 10 drops of liquid dish detergent.
3. Once the yeast blooms, or wakes up, have the students add it to the mixture in the bottle, and watch what happens!
4. Then, have the students draw what they see in the box on the lab report sheet on SL p. 71.

Explanation

The students should see that the mixture bubbles up, creating a foam that pushes up and out of the bottle. Hydrogen peroxide breaks down into water and oxygen naturally, but the reaction is quite slow. An enzyme in yeast, catalase, speeds up this reaction. The dish soap traps the oxygen bubbles, creating the foam that is pushed up and out of the bottle!

Take It Further

Have the students repeat the experiment, only this time do not add yeast. Observe how this changes the results. (The bubbles will still form because the hydrogen peroxide is still breaking down into water and oxygen. but this will happen at a much slower rate.)

(Optional) STEAM Projects

Multi-chapter Activities

✂ PERIODIC TABLE PROJECT – This chapter, there is nothing to add to the periodic table.

Activities For This Chapter

✂ BREATHING FLAME – Have the students see how fire requires oxygen. You will need a candle, a match, and a glass jar. (***Adults Only***) Use the match to light the candle, and have the students observe the flame. Then, turn the jar upside down, and place it over the candle. Have the students observe what happens. (The students should see the flame burn for a bit and then go out. This is because the oxygen that is trapped inside of the jar is used up by the flame. Once it is gone, the flame goes out.)

✂ NITROGEN CYCLE – Have the students learn more about the nitrogen cycle by watching the following video:

🖱 https://www.youtube.com/watch?v=ZaFVfHftzpI

If you would like for your students to also learn about the phosphorus cycle, you can have them watch the following video:

🖱 https://www.youtube.com/watch?v=wdAzQSuypCk

Chapter 14: Grid Schedule

	Supplies Needed
Demo	• 2 Eggs, Toothpaste with fluoride, Plastic wrap, White vinegar, 2 Cups Permanent marker
Projects	• 2 Colors of paint, Paper, A few pom-pom balls, Pencil eraser

Chapter Summary

The chapter opens with the entrance of Tom, a former colleague of the Unseen One, who reveals that the Carboxynitro Games aren't a real competition sanctioned by the Twin Biodomes. Moments later, the twins are flushed through the biodomes' waterslides and end up in a place where they can enter their data and move onto the next location—Chile. They land in a cage with a strange animal that turns out to be a llama. Even so, they can overhear their local expert, Rose Rock, as she shares with the village children about halogens. They also learn about bonding and about the race—the one that Ring Finger, the War Lord King of the Atacama is forcing the villagers to have to get the supplies they need. We learn more about Rose's history as the chief's college-educated daughter and meet her friend Vincent, who happens to be deaf. The chapter ends with Rose pleading with the villagers to race and race to win.

Weekly Schedule

	Day 1	Day 2	Day 3	Day 4
Read	☐ Read the section entitled "Fortuneless Halogens" of Chapter 14 in *SSA Volume 7: Chemistry*.	☐ Read the section entitled "Chemical Bonding" of Chapter 14 in *SSA Volume 7: Chemistry*.	☐ *(Optional)* Read one or all of the assigned pages from the encyclopedia of your choice.	☐ *(Optional)* Read one of the additional library books.
Write	☐ Fill out the Periodic Table Group Sheet on SL p. 77 on halogens. ☐ Go over the vocabulary word and enter it into the Chemistry Glossary on SL p. 107.	☐ Fill out a Chemistry Record Sheet on SL p. 78 on bonding. ☐ *(Optional)* Work on the Chile Map Sheet on SL p. 83.	☐ *(Optional)* Write narration on the Chemistry Notes Sheet on SL p. 84. ☐ Fill out the lab report sheet for the demonstration on SL p. 81.	☐ *(Optional)* Complete the copywork or dictation assignment and add it to the Chemistry Notes Sheet on SL p. 84. ☐ *(Optional)* Fill out the record sheet on SL p. 86 for one of the projects.
Do	☐ *(Optional)* Watch the video on halogens.	☐ *(Optional)* Make some bonding art.	☐ Do the demonstration entitled "Fluoride Help."	☐ Work on the Periodic Table model.

Chapter 14: List schedule

Chapter Summary

The chapter opens with the entrance of Tom, a former colleague of the Unseen One, who reveals that the Carboxynitro Games aren't a real competition sanctioned by the Twin Biodomes. Moments later, the twins are flushed through the biodomes' waterslides and end up in a place where they can enter their data and move onto the next location—Chile. They land in a cage with a strange animal that turns out to be a llama. Even so, they can overhear their local expert, Rose Rock, as she shares with the village children about halogens. They also learn about bonding and about the race—the one that Ring Finger, the War Lord King of the Atacama is forcing the villagers to have to get the supplies they need. We learn more about Rose's history as the chief's college-educated daughter and meet her friend Vincent, who happens to be deaf. The chapter ends with Rose pleading with the villagers to race and race to win.

Essential To-Do's

Read
- ☐ Read the section entitled "Fortuneless Halogens" of Chapter 14 in *SSA Volume 7: Chemistry*.
- ☐ Read the section entitled "Chemical Bonding" of Chapter 14 in *SSA Volume 7: Chemistry*.

Write
- ☐ Fill out the Periodic Table Group Sheet on SL p. 77 on halogens.
- ☐ Fill out a Chemistry Record Sheet on SL p. 78 on bonding.
- ☐ Fill out the lab report sheet for the demonstration on SL p. 81.
- ☐ Go over the vocabulary word and enter it into the Chemistry Glossary on SL p. 107.

Do
- ☐ Do the demonstration entitled "Fluoride Help."
- ☐ Work on the Periodic Table model.

Optional Extras

Read
- ☐ Read one or all of the assigned pages from the encyclopedia of your choice.
- ☐ Read one of the additional library books.

Write
- ☐ Write a narration on the Chemistry Notes Sheet on SL p. 84.
- ☐ Complete the copywork or dictation assignment and add it to the Chemistry Notes Sheet on SL p. 84.
- ☐ Fill out the record sheet on SL p. 86 for one of the projects.
- ☐ Work on the Chile Map Sheet on SL p. 83.

Do
- ☐ Watch the video on halogens.
- ☐ Make some bonding art.

Supplies Needed	
Demo	• 2 Eggs, Toothpaste with fluoride, Plastic wrap, White vinegar, 2 Cups, Permanent marker
Projects	• 2 Colors of paint, Paper, A few pom-pom balls, Pencil eraser

Chapter 14: Iron Nails in Chilean Desert

READ: Gathering Information

Living Book Spine
- Chapter 14 of *The Sassafras Science Adventures Volume 7: Chemistry*

(Optional) Encyclopedia Readings
- *DK Eyewitness: The Elements* p. 63 (Fluorine), p. 64 (Bromine)
- *Scholastic's The Periodic Table* pp. 182-183 (Halogens), p. 184 (Fluorine), p. 188 (Bromine)
- *Usborne Science Encyclopedia* pp. 68-71 (Bonding)
- *Kingfisher Science Encyclopedia* pp. 166-167 (Bonding and Valency)

(Optional) Additional Library Books
- *Learn about Halogens with Bearific® (Bearific® Learning Series)* by Katelyn Lonas
- *Fluorine (Understanding the Elements of the Periodic Table)* by Heather Hasan

WRITE: Keeping a Notebook

SCIDAT Logbook Sheets

This chapter, you can have the students work on the map sheet. You can also have them fill out the record sheets for halogens and bonding along with adding to the notes sheet and glossary. The students should also complete a lab report sheet, and if they want, they can do a project record sheet. Here is the information they could include:

Chile Map Sheet

This chapter, you can have the students look up the minerals found in Chile. Here are a few possibilities:

- Copper
- Iodine
- Iron
- Lithium
- Molybdenum
- Rhenium
- Sodium

Here are two websites you can check out:
- https://www.britannica.com/place/Chile/Mineral-resources-noncarboniferous
- https://www.trade.gov/country-commercial-guides/chile-mining

Periodic Table Group Sheet - Halogens

Elements Included
- Fluorine
- Chlorine
- Bromine
- Iodine
- Astatine
- Tennessine

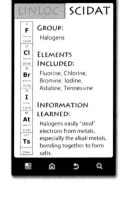

Interesting Information
- The halogens include all the elements from group 17 on the periodic table. These are fluorine, chlorine, bromine, iodine, astatine, and tennessine.
- These elements are all nonmetals, and they react strongly. They easily "steal" electrons from metals, especially the alkali metals, bonding together to form salts. The name halogen literally means "salt giver."
- The halogens often appear as brightly colored gases, liquids, or solids when by themselves. For example, fluorine is a yellow gas, chlorine is a green gas, bromine is a purplish liquid, and iodine is a purple-black solid.
- Fluorine was used during World War 2 in different weapons, but an ion of this halogen, fluoride, is used to strengthen teeth! Many countries add fluoride to their water.
- The Phoenicians were the first known to use a purple dye from sea snails—it turns out that this dye gets its color from the halogen, bromine. This element is also used in making furniture flame resistant.
- Astatine is one of the rarest elements on Earth because it is so radioactive and unstable. It wasn't isolated until 1940.
- Tennessine, also known as element 117, is the second-heaviest element in the world. It is not a natural element and has been only briefly created in the lab.

Chemistry Record Sheet - Bonding

Information Learned
- In chemistry, atoms form molecules by bonding together with other atoms.
- All atoms want to be stable, which means that they have a full house of electrons. Some atoms are like this naturally, like helium. Most are not, and this is why atoms bond with each other—to give each other a full house of electrons. They can do this by donating and receiving electrons or by sharing them.
- There are three main types of bonds:
  1. Ionic Bonding – In ionic bonding, one atom, usually a metal, donates an electron, whereas another atom, usually a nonmetal, receives it. This results in a positively charged ion, the one that gave an electron away, and a negatively charged ion, the one that took the electron. The two ions are then attracted to each other and stay together because of the charge that was created. This is the type of bond that halogens love to make.
  2. Covalent Bonding – In covalent bonding, two or more atoms get together to share electrons so that they can all have a full house together. They can share one pair of electrons to form a single bond or two pairs of electrons to form a double bond, and so on. The atoms that make these types of bonds are typically nonmetals.
  3. Metallic Bonding – In metallic bonding, metal atoms line up together, and then their electrons float around in between them. These mobile electrons are what makes metals good conductors of electricity and heat.
- The way a molecule bonds together determines the properties of that molecule.

Chemistry Notes - Deposition

The following is information that the students could add to their notes page:
- Minerals can be left behind when groundwater leaches into areas near the water table. When it recedes, it can leave behind, or deposit, minerals. These minerals have to be dug out, or mined, from the desert.
- Minerals can be deposited in the desert through evaporation. Rain falls, and as it evaporates in the sun and heat, minerals are left behind. These minerals can be found close to the surface of the desert sand.

Vocabulary

Have the older students look up the following terms in the glossary in the appendix on pp. 133-134 or in a science encyclopedia. Then, have them copy each definition onto a blank index card or into their SCIDAT logbook.

- **Chemical Bond** – A force that holds together two or more atoms.

(Optional) Copywork

Copywork Sentence

The halogen elements are all nonmetals, and they react strongly.

Dictation Selection

The halogens include all the elements from group 17 on the periodic table. These elements are all nonmetals, and they react strongly. They easily "steal" electrons from metals, especially the alkali metals, bonding together to form salts. The name halogen literally means "salt giver." The halogens often appear as brightly colored gases, liquids, or solids when all by themselves.

Do: Playing with Science

Scientific Demonstration: Fluoride Help*

*NOTE—This demonstration needs to be started the night before.

Materials
- ☑ 2 Eggs
- ☑ Toothpaste with fluoride
- ☑ Plastic wrap
- ☑ White vinegar
- ☑ 2 Cups
- ☑ Permanent marker

Procedure
1. Have the students coat one of the eggs with the toothpaste, wrap it in plastic wrap, and set it in the fridge overnight.
2. After 24 hours, gently rinse off any excess toothpaste with warm water, and mark the egg with an "F" using a permanent maker.
3. Then, set both eggs in a cup, and cover them with vinegar.
4. After 30 minutes, check the eggs, and observe what happens. Have the students draw what they see in

the box on the lab report sheet on SL p. 81.
5. Let the eggs sit in the cups overnight. The next morning, take the eggs out and compare the differences. Have the students draw what they see once more on the lab report sheet.

Explanation

The students should see that the egg marked with an "F" does not dissolve nearly as quickly as the one without. Vinegar is an acid that dissolves the calcium in the eggshell. Fluorine is often used in toothpaste to help protect the enamel on teeth, which contains calcium, from being dissolved. In this demonstration, the fluoride in the toothpaste helped protect the treated eggshell from the vinegar and slow the damaging reaction.

Take It Further

Have the students repeat the demonstrations with several different types of toothpaste to see if the results are different.

(Optional) STEAM Projects

Multi-chapter Activities

- **PERIODIC TABLE PROJECT** – This chapter, the students will add the halogens on SL p. 111 to their periodic table poster on SL p. 5.

Activities For This Chapter

- **HALOGENS** – Have the students watch the following video showing the different reactivities of the halogens:
  - https://www.youtube.com/watch?v=saLvwX3_p1s

- **BONDING ART** – Have the students learn about bonding by creating an artistic representation of the different types of bonds. You will need two colors of paint, paper, a few pom-pom balls, and a pencil eraser. Here are the directions:
  - **IONIC BONDING** – Have the students dip a pom-pom in one color of paint and use it to make nine dots in two circles, two in a center circle and seven in a surrounding circle, leaving space for one more in the outer circle. Now take another pom-pom and dip it in the other color of paint to make a dot in the space left in the outer circle you previously made, creating an artistic ionic bond.
  - **COVALENT BONDING** – Have the students dip a pom-pom into one of the colors of paint and use it to make ten dots in two circles, two in a center circle and eight in a surrounding circle. Then, have them cut a pom-pom in half and dip it into the other color of paint. Use the half pom-pom to paint over half of the two of the dots in the outer circle they made previously, creating an artistic covalent bond.
  - **METALLIC BONDING** – Have the students dip a pom-pom into one of the colors of paint and then make a 4-by-3 grid on the paper. (Be sure to leave space in the grid for the mini-dots.) Then, have them dip the end of the pencil eraser into the other color of paint and use it to randomly scatter the mini-dots in within grid they made previously, creating an artistic metallic bond.

Chapter 15: Grid Schedule

Supplies Needed

Demo	• Small piece of potato or a piece of bread, Iodine swab
Projects	• Iodine, Water, Cup, Vitamin C • Shallow pan, Tincture of iodine, Water, Paper, Q-tip, Lemon juice, Cup

Chapter Summary

The chapter opens with Blaine and Tracey remaining undetected in the crate with the llama. From their vantage point, they can see the race buggy the villagers built. The twins realize that there is a catapult on the back of the vehicle just as Rose tells a little village boy about chlorine. As she finishes, the twins feel the crate being hoisted up and taken over to be attached to the catapult on the buggy! Back on Pecan Street, Paul Sims has decided to help with Uncle Cecil's preparations for his dinner with Summer. They are at the Left-handed Turtle Market when genius strikes and Cecil knows what to serve for the meal—sandwiches! Back in Chile, the twins watch as the race begins. They see 12 other homemade dune buggies, including one by a man named Maximiliano, who antagonizes Rose Rock. We flash back to Pecan Street and the Man With No Eyebrows, who has decided that he is going to rebuild the giant Forget-O-Nator and use it to erase everyone's memories. Back in the desert, Rose and Maximiliano are the two leaders of the race. So far, 8 of the other dune buggies have been so damaged that they had to drop out. The crate with the twins is launched, and the next thing Blaine and Tracey hear is information about iodine. Rose apologizes for launching them with the llama crate. The chapter ends with them all getting back on the buggy to finish the race.

Weekly Schedule

	Day 1	Day 2	Day 3	Day 4
Read	☐ Read the section entitled "Chlorine Buggies" of Chapter 15 in *SSA Volume 7: Chemistry*.	☐ Read the section entitled "Healing Iodine" of Chapter 15 in *SSA Volume 7: Chemistry*.	☐ (*Optional*) Read one or all of the assigned pages from the encyclopedia of your choice.	☐ (*Optional*) Read one of the additional library books.
Write	☐ Fill out an Element Record Sheet on SL p. 79 on chlorine. ☐ Go over the vocabulary word and enter it into the Chemistry Glossary on SL p. 108.	☐ Fill out an Element Record Sheet on SL p. 80 on iodine. ☐ (*Optional*) Work on the Chile Map Sheet on SL p. 83.	☐ (*Optional*) Write narration on the Chemistry Notes Sheet on SL p. 85. ☐ Fill out the lab report sheet for the demonstration on SL p. 82.	☐ (*Optional*) Complete the copywork or dictation assignment and add it to the Chemistry Notes Sheet on SL p. 85. ☐ (*Optional*) Fill out the record sheet on SL p. 87 for one of the projects. ☐ (*Optional*) Take Chemistry Quiz #7.
Do	☐ (*Optional*) Do the Iodine and Vitamin C activity.	☐ (*Optional*) Pass along a secret message.	☐ Do the demonstration entitled "Iodine Test."	

Chapter 15: List schedule

Chapter Summary

The chapter opens with Blaine and Tracey remaining undetected in the crate with the llama. From their vantage point, they can see the race buggy the villagers built. The twins realize that there is a catapult on the back of the vehicle just as Rose tells a little village boy about chlorine. As she finishes, the twins feel the crate being hoisted up and taken over to be attached to the catapult on the buggy! Back on Pecan Street, Paul Sims has decided to help with Uncle Cecil's preparations for his dinner with Summer. They are at the Left-handed Turtle Market when genius strikes and Cecil knows what to serve for the meal—sandwiches! Back in Chile, the twins watch as the race begins. They see 12 other homemade dune buggies, including one by a man named Maximiliano, who antagonizes Rose Rock. We flash back to Pecan Street and the Man With No Eyebrows, who has decided that he is going to rebuild the giant Forget-O-Nator and use it to erase everyone's memories. Back in the desert, Rose and Maximiliano are the two leaders of the race. So far, 8 of the other dune buggies have been so damaged that they had to drop out. The crate with the twins is launched, and the next thing Blaine and Tracey hear is information about iodine. Rose apologizes for launching them with the llama crate. The chapter ends with them all getting back on the buggy to finish the race.

Essential To-Do's

Read
- ☐ Read the section entitled "Chlorine Buggies" of Chapter 15 in *SSA Volume 7: Chemistry*.
- ☐ Read the section entitled "Healing Iodine" of Chapter 15 in *SSA Volume 7: Chemistry*.

Write
- ☐ Fill out an Element Record Sheet on SL p. 79 on chlorine.
- ☐ Fill out an Element Record Sheet on SL p. 80 on iodine.
- ☐ Fill out the lab report sheet for the demonstration on SL p. 82.
- ☐ Go over the vocabulary word and enter it into the Chemistry Glossary on SL p. 108.

Do
- ☐ Do the demonstration entitled "Iodine Test."

Optional Extras

Read
- ☐ Read one or all of the assigned pages from the encyclopedia of your choice.
- ☐ Read one of the additional library books.

Write
- ☐ Write a narration on the Chemistry Notes Sheet on SL p. 85.
- ☐ Complete the copywork or dictation assignment and add it to the Chemistry Notes Sheet on SL p. 85.
- ☐ Fill out the record sheet on SL p. 87 for one of the projects.
- ☐ Work on the Chile Map Sheet on SL p. 83.
- ☐ Take Chemistry Quiz #7.

Do
- ☐ Do the Iodine and Vitamin C activity.
- ☐ Pass along a secret message.

Supplies Needed	
Demo	• Small piece of potato or a piece of bread, Iodine swab
Projects	• Iodine, Water, Cup, Vitamin C • Shallow pan, Tincture of iodine, Water, Paper, Q-tip, Lemon juice, Cup

The Sassafras Guide to Chemistry ~ Chapter 15

Chapter 15: The Desert Dune Buggy Race

Read: Gathering Information

Living Book Spine
- Chapter 15 of *The Sassafras Science Adventures Volume 7: Chemistry*

(Optional) Encyclopedia Readings
- *DK Eyewitness: The Elements* p. 62 (Chlorine), p. 65 (Remaining Halogens)
- *Scholastic's The Periodic Table* p. 185 (Chlorine), p. 189 (Remaining Halogens)
- *Usborne Science Encyclopedia* pp. 48-49 (Halogens)
- *Kingfisher Science Encyclopedia* pp. 182 (The Halogens)

(Optional) Additional Library Books
- *Chlorine (True Books)* by Salvatore Tocci
- *The Elements: Iodine* by Leon Gray
- *Iodine (Understanding the Elements of the Periodic Table)* by Kristi Lew

Write: Keeping a Notebook

SCIDAT Logbook Sheets

This chapter, you can have the students work on the map sheet. You can also have them fill out the record sheets for chlorine and iodine along with adding to the notes sheet and glossary. The students should also complete a lab report sheet, and if they want, they can do a project record sheet. Here is the information they could include:

Chile Map Sheet

This chapter, you can have the students look up the industry found in Chile. Here are a few possibilities:

- Hydroelectric
- Coal
- Gas
- Oil

Here are pages from the suggested atlas you can read:

- *DK Children's Illustrated Atlas* pp. 30-31 (Argentina and Chile)

Element Record Sheet - Chlorine

Information Learned
- Chlorine is very reactive, so it's not found on its own in nature. Instead, it's mainly found in salt compounds, like sodium chloride.
- The symbol for chlorine is Cl. The atomic number for chlorine is 17, and the atomic mass is 35.45.
- The poison dart frog secretes a chlorine-containing compound as part of its defense.

- Chlorine is a greenish gas that is very toxic. In fact, it was used as a chemical weapon during World War 1.
- Chlorine compounds in small amounts help make water safe to drink because it is deadly to bacteria and viruses. It is found in bleach.
- Chlorine is another trace mineral that we need in our bodies. It helps with digestion, muscle movement, and immunity.
- Chlorine is also used to make PVC, which is a lightweight and strong plastic used for pipes, windows, and so much more.

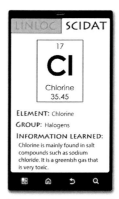

Element Record Sheet - Iodine

Information Learned

- Iodine is almost never seen on its own. It is usually paired together with itself or with another element to form a compound.
- The symbol for iodine is I. The atomic number for iodine is 53, and the atomic mass is 126.9.
- Iodine is usually a blackish purple solid. It is named after the Greek word, *iodes*, which means violet.
- However, when iodine is heated, it turns quickly into a purplish gas without becoming a liquid. This process is called sublimation, which is when a solid turns directly into a gas.
- Compounds with iodine are found is seawater and fish.
- Another iodine-containing compound is used to treat cuts and during surgery as an antiseptic. This yellow-brown liquid can sting, but it is effective at preventing infections. This same iodine-containing liquid is used in starch tests because it turns blue-black in the presence of starch.
- Iodine is a trace mineral necessary for humans, which is why it is often added to table salt. Our bodies use this halogen for help in making hormones in the thyroid.

Chemistry Notes - Electrolysis

The following is information that the students could add to their notes page:

- Electrolysis is method of separating compounds by passing an electrical current through a solution with the compound.
- Chlorine gas is produced through electrolysis of a sodium chloride brine solution.

Vocabulary

Have the older students look up the following terms in the glossary in the appendix on pp. 133-134 or in a science encyclopedia. Then, have them copy each definition onto a blank index card or into their SCIDAT logbook.

- ION – An atom or group of atoms that has become charged by gaining or losing one or more electrons.

(Optional) Copywork

Copywork Sentence

Both chlorine and iodine are trace minerals that the body needs.

Dictation Selection

Iodine is usually a blackish purple solid. However, when iodine is heated up, it turns quickly into a purplish gas without becoming a liquid. This process is called sublimation, which is when a solid turns directly into a gas.

(Optional) Quiz

This chapter, you can give the students a quiz based on what they learned in Chapters 14 and 15. You can find the quiz in the appendix on p. 155.

Quiz #7 Answers
1. B,A
2. True
3. False (The elements in the halogens group are very reactive.)
4. Chlorine
5. True
6. Electrolysis
7. Ionic, Metallic, Covalent

Do: Playing with Science

Scientific Demonstration: Iodine Test

Materials
- ☑ Small piece of potato or a piece of bread
- ☑ Iodine swab

Procedure
1. Have students swab the food sample with the iodine swab and watch what happens.
2. Then, have the students draw what they saw in the box on the lab report sheet on SL p. 82.

Explanation
The students should see the iodine will change to blue-purple in the presence of a starch. Both bread and potatoes have starch in them.

Take It Further
Have the students test other foods for the presence of starch. (Iodine is brown-black normally, but will change to blue-purple in the presence of a starch.)

(Optional) STEAM Projects

Multi-chapter Activities
✂ PERIODIC TABLE PROJECT – This chapter, there is nothing to add to the periodic table.

Activities For This Chapter
✂ IODINE AND VITAMIN C – Have the students do a magic disappearing coloring activity using iodine, water, a cup, and vitamin C. You can see the directions for this project here:
  🖱 https://www.steamsational.com/iodine-and-vitamin-c-experiment/

✂ SECRET MESSAGE – Have the students use iodine to reveal a secret message. You will need a shallow pan, tincture of iodine, water, paper, Q-tip, lemon juice, and a cup. Pour some lemon juice into a cup. Then, have the students use the lemon juice and Q-tip to write a message on the paper. Meanwhile, mix together a cup of water and 20 drops of tincture of iodine in the bowl until well mixed. Once the juice has dried on the paper, have the students give you the sheet. Place it into the iodine solution in the pan to reveal the message!

Chapter 16: Grid Schedule

Supplies Needed	
Demo	• Helium-filled balloon, Scissors
Projects	• No additional supplies needed

Chapter Summary

The chapter opens with a photo finish. Maximiliano wins. In a surprising twist, the decides to share his winnings with all the villagers. Ring Finger is furious, but that lasts only moments as he quickly realizes that the villagers are standing up to him and the police are there to arrest him. After several hours, the twins find themselves alone with time to enter their data and head off to the next location—Morocco. Back on Pecan Street, Paul is convincing Uncle Cecil that his ideas are better that Cecil's and Cecil should let him prepare the dinner for Summer. Back in Morocco, Blaine and Tracey land in a crate again. They overhear a conversation about noble gases, helium, and an escape. The twins are soon discovered by the people having the conversation, and they meet their location experts—the SAM Collective. Samirah, Samir, and Sami explain how they were taken by the anonymous snake-charmers of Morocco and how they are going to escape over the Atlas Mountains in a homemade hot-air balloon. The chapter ends with the SAM Collective insisting that the twins come with them.

Weekly Schedule

	Day 1	Day 2	Day 3	Day 4
Read	☐ Read the section entitled "Mysterious Noble Gases" of Chapter 16 in *SSA Volume 7: Chemistry*.	☐ Read the section entitled "Gaseous Helium" of Chapter 16 in *SSA Volume 7: Chemistry*.	☐ (*Optional*) Read one or all of the assigned pages from the encyclopedia of your choice.	☐ (*Optional*) Read one of the additional library books.
Write	☐ Fill out the Periodic Table Group Sheet on SL p. 88 on noble gases. ☐ Go over the vocabulary word and enter it into the Chemistry Glossary on SL p. 108.	☐ Fill out an Element Record Sheet on SL p. 89 on helium. ☐ (*Optional*) Work on the Morocco Map Sheet on SL p. 94.	☐ (*Optional*) Write narration on the Chemistry Notes Sheet on SL p. 95. ☐ Fill out the lab report sheet for the demonstration on SL p. 92.	☐ (*Optional*) Complete the copywork or dictation assignment and add it to the Chemistry Notes Sheet on SL p. 92. ☐ (*Optional*) Fill out the record sheet on SL p. 96 for one of the projects.
Do	☐ (*Optional*) Learn about a Dangerous Noble Gas.	☐ (*Optional*) Learn about Helium's History.	☐ Do the demonstration entitled "Funny Voice."	☐ Work on the Periodic Table model.

Chapter 16: List Schedule

Chapter Summary

The chapter opens with a photo finish. Maximiliano wins. In a surprising twist, the decides to share his winnings with all the villagers. Ring Finger is furious, but that lasts only moments as he quickly realizes that the villagers are standing up to him and the police are there to arrest him. After several hours, the twins find themselves alone with time to enter their data and head off to the next location—Morocco. Back on Pecan Street, Paul is convincing Uncle Cecil that his ideas are better that Cecil's and Cecil should let him prepare the dinner for Summer. Back in Morocco, Blaine and Tracey land in a crate again. They overhear a conversation about noble gases, helium, and an escape. The twins are soon discovered by the people having the conversation, and they meet their location experts—the SAM Collective. Samirah, Samir, and Sami explain how they were taken by the anonymous snake-charmers of Morocco and how they are going to escape over the Atlas Mountains in a homemade hot-air balloon. The chapter ends with the SAM Collective insisting that the twins come with them.

Essential To-Do's

Read
- ☐ Read the section entitled "Mysterious Noble Gases" of Chapter 16 in *SSA Volume 7: Chemistry*.
- ☐ Read the section entitled "Gaseous Helium" of Chapter 16 in *SSA Volume 7: Chemistry*.

Write
- ☐ Fill out the Periodic Table Group Sheet on SL p. 88 on noble gases.
- ☐ Fill out an Element Record Sheet on SL p. 89 on helium.
- ☐ Fill out the lab report sheet for the demonstration on SL p. 92.
- ☐ Go over the vocabulary word and enter it into the Chemistry Glossary on SL p. 108.

Do
- ☐ Do the demonstration entitled "Funny Voice."
- ☐ Work on the Periodic Table model.

Optional Extras

Read
- ☐ Read one or all of the assigned pages from the encyclopedia of your choice.
- ☐ Read one of the additional library books.

Write
- ☐ Write a narration on the Chemistry Notes Sheet on SL p. 95.
- ☐ Complete the copywork or dictation assignment and add it to the Chemistry Notes Sheet on SL p. 95.
- ☐ Fill out the record sheet on SL p. 96 for one of the projects.
- ☐ Work on the Morocco Map Sheet on SL p. 94.

Do
- ☐ Learn about a Dangerous Noble Gas.
- ☐ Learn about Helium's History.

Supplies Needed	
Demo	• Helium-filled balloon, Scissors
Projects	• No additional supplies needed

Chapter 16: On to Morocco

Read: Gathering Information

Living Book Spine
- Chapter 16 of *The Sassafras Science Adventures Volume 7: Chemistry*

(Optional) Encyclopedia Readings
- *DK Eyewitness: The Elements* p. 66 (Helium), pp. 68-69 (Remaining Noble Gases)
- *Scholastic's The Periodic Table* pp. 190-191 (Noble Gases), p. 192 (Helium)
- *Usborne Science Encyclopedia* p. 63 (section on Nobel Gases)
- *Kingfisher Science Encyclopedia* p. 180 (Nobel Gases)

(Optional) Additional Library Books
- *Hydrogen and the Noble Gases (True Books: Elements)* by Salvatore Tocci
- *Hooray for Helium!: Understanding the 2nd Most Common Element (The Chem Kids)* by Blake Washington and Mallette Pagano

Write: Keeping a Notebook

SCIDAT Logbook Sheets

This chapter, you can have the students work on the map sheet. You can also have them fill out the record sheets for noble gases and helium along with adding to the notes sheet and glossary. The students should also complete a lab report sheet, and if they want, they can do a project record sheet. Here is the information they could include:

Morocco Map Sheet

This chapter, you can have the students look up the minerals found in Morocco. Here are a few possibilities:

- Phosphates
- Iron
- Manganese
- Lead
- Zinc

Here are two websites you can check out:
- https://www.britannica.com/place/Morocco/Economy#ref46576
- https://www.azomining.com/Article.aspx?ArticleID=186

Periodic Table Group Sheet - Noble Gases

Elements Included
- Helium
- Neon
- Argon

- Krypton
- Xenon
- Radon
- Oganesson

Interesting Information
- The noble gases include all the elements from group 18 on the far right of the periodic table. These are helium, neon, argon, krypton, xenon, radon, and oganesson.
- These elements are all nonmetals, and they are considered inert, meaning they don't react chemically or combine with other elements. This is because they have a full outer shell of electrons. The rare exception is xenon, which will make a few compounds.
- Many of the noble gases are found in the atmosphere.
- Argon was the first noble gas to be discovered. It was found by Scottish chemist, William Ramsay, who separated it from liquid air in 1894. He was also a part of discovering krypton gas, another noble gas, in 1898 along with Morris Travers, an English chemist. On top of that, in 1904, William Ramsay was awarded the Nobel Prize in chemistry for discovering five noble gases—helium, neon, argon, krypton, and xenon.
- Argon is named after the Greek word for lazy because it is so inactive. It is used to create a safe atmosphere for arc welding and as insulation between windowpanes.
- Krypton is named after the Greek word for hidden because it was so hard to find. It is used in fluorescent lights and in monitors for radioactive elements.
- Xenon is used in light bulbs, giving off a blue glow. It is also used to sterilize surfaces and as a propellant in ion thrusters.
- Radon is produced when uranium and thorium decay. It's a heavy gas that can be toxic in high quantities.
- Oganesson is a lab-created noble gas that is thought to be similar to radon. It was made in 2002.
- When Mendeleev created his periodic table, he did not predict the existence of the noble gases as a group of elements, even though he did say other elements would be found.

Element Record Sheet - Helium
Information Learned
- Helium is a colorless, tasteless gas with no smell, so even though it's present in the atmosphere, you don't know it's there!
- The symbol for helium is He. The atomic number for helium is 2, and the atomic mass is 4.003.
- Helium is a noble gas that is lighter than air, so it is often used to blow up balloons. It's also the gas that will give you a squeaky voice if you inhale it.
- Helium makes up about a quarter of the weight in the universe. It is produced in massive stars when four hydrogen atoms fuse together, releasing tons of energy.
- On Earth, helium is used in weather balloons and airships.
- Helium is also used in welding because it is so inert, or unreactive.
- Liquid helium is used as a coolant for superconducting magnets in MRI machines.

Chemistry Notes - There are no additional topics this chapter.

Vocabulary
Have the older students look up the following term in the glossary in the appendix on pp. 133-134 or in

a science encyclopedia. Then, have them copy each definition onto a blank index card or into their SCIDAT logbook.

> ✂ INERT – An element that is completely nonreactive.

(Optional) Copywork

Copywork Sentence
Many of the noble gases are found in the atmosphere.

Dictation Selection
The noble gases include all the elements from group 18 on the far right of the periodic table. These elements are all nonmetals, and they are considered inert, meaning they really don't react chemically or combine with other elements. This is because they have a full outer shell of electrons.

Do: Playing with Science

Scientific Demonstration: Funny Voice

Materials
- ☑ Helium-filled balloon
- ☑ Scissors

Procedure
(CAUTION - Helium is nontoxic, but it can cause light-headedness. Do NOT let the students do this activity—you need to demonstrate it for them. Do NOT repeat it more than once, and be sure to follow the directions.)

1. Pinch the base of a helium-filled balloon under the knot, and cut off the end so that you can get some of the gas to release.
2. Exhale completely and place the cut balloon under your chin.
3. As you inhale, open the balloon so that you breathe in some of the helium. Then, start to talk or sing so that the students can observe the difference in your voice.
4. Then, have the students fill out the lab report sheet on SL p. 92.

Explanation
The students should observe that your voice now has a squeaky quality to it and may even seem to be a bit higher. This is because helium is six times lighter than air, so the sound waves of your voice speed up as they pass through the gas, causing your voice to sound squeaky.

Take It Further
There is no "Take It Further" activity for this chapter.

(Optional) STEAM Projects

Multi-chapter Activities
- ✂ PERIODIC TABLE PROJECT – This chapter, the students will add the noble gases on SL p. 111 to their periodic table poster on SL p. 5.

Activities For This Chapter

- **DANGEROUS NOBLE GAS** – Radon is a noble gas that is one of the products of radioactive decay. It can build up in the basements of homes that sit over natural deposits of thorium or uranium. If there is radon present in a house, contractors can install a system that flushes it out. See if you live in radon zone:

    http://www.epa.gov/radon/epa-map-radon-zones

- **HELIUM'S HISTORY** – Have the students learn more about the history of helium-filled blimps by watching the following video:

    https://www.youtube.com/watch?v=vfpv6JXMaGM

Chapter 17: Grid Schedule

Supplies Needed	
Demo	• Small cup, Tissue paper, Water, Bucket or large bowl
Projects	• Candle, Bottle, Baking soda, Vinegar

Chapter Summary

The chapter opens with a lot of flashing between perspectives. President Lincoln is upset about what Paul Sims is doing with Uncle Cecil's plans. The Man With No Eyebrows has fixed the Forget-O-Nator bus. Paul Sims has a plan to get in good with Cecil and Summer to avoid suspicion from the Swiss Secret Service. Summer is completing her paperwork right before she zips off to Pecan Street. Yang Bo is leaving the International Space Station and heading back to Earth. Blaine and Tracey are flying high in a homemade hot-air balloon. The group has escaped and are now heading towards Marrakesh. The twins fall asleep, and when they wake up the hot-air balloon is approaching the city, which is full of bright lights. The SAM Collective shares with the twins about neon and air as they float over the city. The group crash-lands in a giant market, right in the middle of a group of snake-charmers. A chase ensues. The chapter ends with a spectacular crash between three familiar backpackers and the people pursuing the twins and the SAM Collective.

Weekly Schedule

	Day 1	Day 2	Day 3	Day 4
Read	☐ Read the section entitled "Neon Outbreak" of Chapter 17 in *SSA Volume 7: Chemistry*.	☐ Read the section entitled "Air Below" of Chapter 17 in *SSA Volume 7: Chemistry*.	☐ *(Optional)* Read one or all of the assigned pages from the encyclopedia of your choice.	☐ *(Optional)* Read one of the additional library books.
Write	☐ Fill out an Element Record Sheet on SL p. 90 on neon. ☐ Go over the vocabulary word and enter it into the Chemistry Glossary on SL p. 108.	☐ Fill out an Element Record Sheet on SL p. 91 on air. ☐ *(Optional)* Work on the Morocco Map Sheet on SL p. 94.	☐ *(Optional)* Write narration on the Chemistry Notes Sheet on SL p. 95. ☐ Fill out the lab report sheet for the demonstration on SL p. 93.	☐ *(Optional)* Complete the copywork or dictation assignment and add it to the Chemistry Notes Sheet on SL p. 95. ☐ *(Optional)* Fill out the record sheet on SL p. 97 for one of the projects. ☐ *(Optional)* Take Chemistry Quiz #8.
Do	☐ *(Optional)* Take a Neon Lights Field Trip.	☐ *(Optional)* Try to put the Air Out!	☐ Do the demonstration entitled "Air in There."	

Chapter 17: List Schedule

Chapter Summary

The chapter opens with a lot of flashing between perspectives. President Lincoln is upset about what Paul Sims is doing with Uncle Cecil's plans. The Man With No Eyebrows has fixed the Forget-O-Nator bus. Paul Sims has a plan to get in good with Cecil and Summer to avoid suspicion from the Swiss Secret Service. Summer is completing her paperwork right before she zips off to Pecan Street. Yang Bo is leaving the International Space Station and heading back to Earth. Blaine and Tracey are flying high in a homemade hot-air balloon. The group has escaped and are now heading towards Marrakesh. The twins fall asleep, and when they wake up the hot-air balloon is approaching the city, which is full of bright lights. The SAM Collective shares with the twins about neon and air as they float over the city. The group crash-lands in a giant market, right in the middle of a group of snake-charmers. A chase ensues. The chapter ends with a spectacular crash between three familiar backpackers and the people pursuing the twins and the SAM Collective.

Essential To-Do's

Read
- ☐ Read the section entitled "Neon Outbreak" of Chapter 17 in *SSA Volume 7: Chemistry*.
- ☐ Read the section entitled "Air Below" of Chapter 17 in *SSA Volume 7: Chemistry*.

Write
- ☐ Fill out an Element Record Sheet on SL p. 90 on neon.
- ☐ Fill out a Chemistry Record Sheet on SL p. 91 on air.
- ☐ Fill out the lab report sheet for the demonstration on SL p. 93.
- ☐ Go over the vocabulary word and enter it into the Chemistry Glossary on SL p. 108.

Do
- ☐ Do the demonstration entitled "Air in There."

Optional Extras

Read
- ☐ Read one or all of the assigned pages from the encyclopedia of your choice.
- ☐ Read one of the additional library books.

Write
- ☐ Write a narration on the Chemistry Notes Sheet on SL p. 95.
- ☐ Complete the copywork or dictation assignment and add it to the Chemistry Notes Sheet on SL p. 95.
- ☐ Fill out the record sheet on SL p. 97 for one of the projects.
- ☐ Work on the Morocco Map Sheet on SL p. 94.
- ☐ Take Chemistry Quiz #8.

Do
- ☐ Take a Neon Lights Field Trip.
- ☐ Try to put the Air Out!

Supplies Needed	
Demo	• Small cup, Tissue paper, Water, Bucket or large bowl
Projects	• Candle, Bottle, Baking soda, Vinegar

Chapter 17: Just a Bunch of Hot Air

Read: Gathering Information

Living Book Spine
- Chapter 17 of *The Sassafras Science Adventures Volume 7: Chemistry*

(Optional) Encyclopedia Readings
- *DK Eyewitness: The Elements* p. 67 (Neon)
- *Scholastic's The Periodic Table* p. 193 (Neon)
- *Usborne Science Encyclopedia* pp. 62-65 (Air)
- *Kingfisher Science Encyclopedia* p. 172 (Air)

(Optional) Additional Library Books
- *Air Is All Around You (Let's-Read-and-Find... Science 1)* by Franklyn M. Branley
- *Air: Outside, Inside, and All Around (Amazing Science)* by Darlene R. Stille

Write: Keeping a Notebook

SCIDAT Logbook Sheets

This chapter, you can have the students work on the map sheet. You can also have them fill out the record sheets for neon and air along with adding to the notes sheet and glossary. The students should also complete a lab report sheet, and if they want, they can do a project record sheet. Here is the information they could include:

Morocco Map Sheet

This chapter, you can have the students look up the industry found in Morocco. Here in one possibility:

- Phosphorite

Here are pages from the suggested atlas you can read:

- *DK Children's Illustrated Atlas* pp. 38-39 (North Africa)

Element Record Sheet - Neon

Information Learned
- Neon is the least reactive element on the whole periodic table. It does not form compounds or react with any other substances.
- The symbol for neon is Ne. The atomic number for neon is 10, and the atomic mass is 20.18.
- Neon comes from the Greek word "*neos*," which means new. It is the fifth-most common element in the universe, but it is rather rare on Earth.
- Neon is a colorless gas except when you pass electricity through it! The gas will glow bright red, and it is often what fills the glass tubes on neon signs.

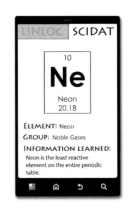

The very first neon light display was in Paris, and it was lit on December 11, 1910.
- Neon is used in television, in fluorescent tubes, and in indicator lights.
- Neon is also used in helium-neon lasers, which are used as barcode scanners in shops.

Chemistry Record Sheet - Air

Information Learned

- Air is a mixture of gases that form a protective layer around the Earth that we call the atmosphere. These gases are held loosely in place by gravity.
- Air protects us from ultraviolet radiation from the sun and is essential to life on Earth.
- It helps plants make their food and gives animals what they need to breathe. In fact, there is enough air to breathe up to 6 miles above the Earth's surface.
- The two main gases in the air are nitrogen and oxygen, but there are traces of carbon dioxide and noble gas elements. Air is 78% nitrogen, 21% oxygen, and 1% other gases.
- Air also holds water vapor, dust, pollen, and pollutants.
- Carbon dioxide in the air traps heat from the sun and keeps the Earth at a temperature that supports life. This is known as the greenhouse effect.

Chemistry Notes - Distillation

The following is information that the students could add to their notes page:
- Noble gases can be separated from the air by fractional distillation.
- Fractional distillation is a process where a mixture, such as air, is separated into its components. This can be done physically, such as heating it, or chemically. Air is cooled and compressed into a liquid, and then as it is heated up again, the different gases are collected.

Vocabulary

Have the older students look up the following term in the glossary in the appendix on pp. 133-134 or in a science encyclopedia. Then, have them copy each definition onto a blank index card or into their SCIDAT logbook.

AIR – A mixture of gases that form a protective layer around the Earth.

(Optional) Copywork

Copywork Sentence

Air is a mixture of gases that surround the Earth.

Dictation Selection

Air is a mixture of gases that form a protective layer around the Earth that we call the atmosphere. Air protects us from ultraviolet radiation from the sun and is essential to life on Earth. It helps plants make their food and gives animals what they need to breathe. In fact, there is enough air to breathe up to 6 miles above the Earth's surface.

(Optional) Quiz

This chapter, you can give the students a quiz based on what they learned in Chapters 16 and 17. You can find the quiz in the appendix on p. 157.

Quiz #8 Answers
1. B,A
2. Least
3. False (Helium is lighter than air.)
4. Excited
5. Nitrogen, Oxygen
6. Liquids

DO: PLAYING WITH SCIENCE

SCIENTIFIC DEMONSTRATION: AIR IN THERE

Materials
- ☑ Small cup
- ☑ Tissue paper
- ☑ Water
- ☑ Bucket or large bowl

Procedure
1. Have the students wad up the tissue paper and smoosh it into the bottom of the cup so that it stays in place when the cup is turned upside down.
2. Meanwhile, fill the bucket about two-thirds of the way full with water.
3. Have the students turn the cup upside down so that the opening faces down to the water.
4. Then, have them push the cup quickly into the water and observe what happens. (NOTE—Be sure to keep the cup completely vertical.)
5. Next, have the students pull the cup straight out of the water without tilting it, observing what happens.
6. Then, have the students fill out the lab report sheet on SL p. 93.

Explanation

The students should see that the paper stays dry when the cup is plunged into the water and taken out again. This is because the cup stays full of air, preventing the water from entering the cup and keeping the paper dry.

Take It Further

Have the students play a game with air. You will need a balloon for this activity. Blow up the balloon, sharing with the students that air is what fills the balloons. Then, hit the balloon back and forth to each other. The goal of the game is to keep the balloon from touching the ground. See how many times you can go back and forth without doing so!

(OPTIONAL) STEAM PROJECTS

Multi-chapter Activities
- ✂ PERIODIC TABLE PROJECT – This chapter, there is nothing to add to the periodic table.

Activities For This Chapter
- ✂ NEON LIGHTS – Head out on field trip to look for neon lights! You may want to read the following article beforehand so that you understand how neon lights work and what elements give

them their color:

- 🖱 http://www.ehow.com/how-does_4927221_neon-its-colors.html

✂ AIR OUT – Have the students test how carbon dioxide puts out a fire. You will need a candle, a bottle, baking soda, and vinegar. The directions for this activity can be found here:

- 🖱 https://www.ronyestech.com/2020/05/how-to-make-carbon-dioxide-gas.html

Chapter 18: Grid Schedule

Supplies Needed	
Demo	• Periodic Table Match-up Cards (free download from Elemental Science)
Projects	• Vegetable oil, Cornstarch, Water, Food coloring, Plastic bag, Eyedropper • White (or clear gel) glue, Water, Plastic baggie, Borax

Chapter Summary

The chapter opens with the twins wondering if Skip, Gannon, and Gretchen, the backpackers they had meant in Peru, were the ones had stopped the chase. Meanwhile, Samirah, Samir, and Sami tell their story to the police. The snake-charmers are arrested, and Blaine and Tracey head back to Uncle Cecil's. They arrive to find a clean basement that looks more like a fancy restaurant than Uncle Cecil's lab. They get their bonus data, and Uncle Cecil appears. The twins find out that the changes are all a part of a dinner for Summer. They are about to find out why when Paul Sims rudely interrupts, explaining how he fixed Cecil's sloppy plans into the amazing setting the twins can see now. Blaine and Tracey learn of their uncle's love equation realization. They encourage their uncle that Summer would have loved his original plan, but Paul Sims will hear none of it. The chapter ends with the sound of Summer T. Beach coming down the trap door slide!

Weekly Schedule

	Day 1	Day 2	Day 3	Day 4
Read	☐ Read the section entitled "Bonus Data" of Chapter 18 in *SSA Volume 7: Chemistry*.	☐ *(Optional)* Read one or all of the assigned pages from the encyclopedia of your choice.	☐ Read the section entitled "A Periodic Setup" of Chapter 18 in *SSA Volume 7: Chemistry*..	
Write	☐ Add information learned about hydrocarbons and polymers to the SL p. 98.	☐ *(Optional)* Write a narration on the Chemistry Notes Sheet on SL p. 99.	☐ *(Optional)* Complete the copywork or dictation assignment and add it to the Chemistry Notes Sheet on SL p. 99.	☐ Review the work you have done over the unit.
Do	☐ *(Optional)* Make a Bioplastic.	☐ Play a game of Periodic Table Match-up.	☐ *(Optional)* Make a Polymer Slime.	

Chapter 18: List Schedule

Chapter Summary

The chapter opens with the twins wondering if Skip, Gannon, and Gretchen, the backpackers they had meant in Peru, were the ones had stopped the chase. Meanwhile, Samirah, Samir, and Sami tell their story to the police. The snake-charmers are arrested, and Blaine and Tracey head back to Uncle Cecil's. They arrive to find a clean basement that looks more like a fancy restaurant than Uncle Cecil's lab. They get their bonus data, and Uncle Cecil appears. The twins find out that the changes are all a part of a dinner for Summer. They are about to find out why when Paul Sims rudely interrupts, explaining how he fixed Cecil's sloppy plans into the amazing setting the twins can see now. Blaine and Tracey learn of their uncle's love equation realization. They encourage their uncle that Summer would have loved his original plan, but Paul Sims will hear none of it. The chapter ends with the sound of Summer T. Beach coming down the trap door slide!

Essential To-Do's

Read
- ☐ Read the section entitled "Bonus Data" of Chapter 18 in *SSA Volume 7: Chemistry*.
- ☐ Read the section entitled "A Periodic Setup" of Chapter 18 in *SSA Volume 7: Chemistry*.

Write
- ☐ Add information learned about hydrocarbons and polymers to the SL p. 98.

Do
- ☐ Play a game of Periodic Table Match-up.
- ☐ Review the work you have done over the unit.

Optional Extras

Read
- ☐ Read one or all of the assigned pages from the encyclopedia of your choice.
- ☐ Read one of the additional library books.

Write
- ☐ Write a narration on the Chemistry Notes Sheet on SL p. 99.
- ☐ Complete the copywork or dictation assignment and add it to the Chemistry Notes Sheet on SL p. 99.

Do
- ☐ Make a Bioplastic.
- ☐ Make a Polymer Slime.

	Supplies Needed
Demo	• Periodic Table Match-up Cards (free download from Elemental Science)
Projects	• Vegetable oil, Cornstarch, Water, Food coloring, Plastic bag, Eyedropper • White (or clear gel) glue, Water, Plastic baggie, Borax

Chapter 18: Zipping Back to Pecan Street

Read: Gathering Information

Living Book Spine
- Chapter 18 of *The Sassafras Science Adventures Volume 7: Chemistry*

(Optional) Encyclopedia Readings
- *DK Eyewitness: The Elements* (no pages scheduled)
- *Scholastic's The Periodic Table* (no pages scheduled)
- *Usborne Science Encyclopedia* pp. 101-102 (Polymers and Plastics)
- *Kingfisher Science Encyclopedia* pp. 174-175 (Organic Chemistry), p. 215 (Polymers)

(Optional) Additional Library Books
- *Plastic (Everyday Materials)* by Andrew Langley
- *Plastic, Ahoy!: Investigating the Great Pacific Garbage Patch* by Patricia Newman and Annie Crawley
- *The Adventures of a Plastic Bottle: A Story About Recycling (Little Green Books)* by Alison Inches and Pete Whitehead
- *From Plastic to Soccer Ball (Start to Finish: Sports Gear)* by Robin Nelson

Write: Keeping a Notebook

SCIDAT Logbook Sheets

This chapter, you can have the students fill the Chemistry Notes Sheets with the bonus data. Here's the information they could include:

Bonus Data - Hydrocarbons
- These molecules are made from mainly hydrogen and carbon.
- Hydrocarbons are combustible, and most are produced by fractional distillation of crude oil.
- Simple hydrocarbons, such as methane, are usually gases, but as the number or carbons increase, the molecules are liquids at room temperature.

Bonus Data - Polymers
- Polymers are substances with long-chain molecules, each made up of many small molecules called monomers.
- There are natural polymers like cellulose and amber.
- There are man-made polymers like nylons, plastic, and PVC. These man-made polymers are cheap to make. They can be soft or hard, as well as pliable or rigid.

Vocabulary

There is no vocabulary to add this chapter.

(Optional) Copywork

Copywork Sentence
Hydrocarbons are made up of hydrogen and carbon.

Dictation Selection
Polymers are substances with long-chain molecules, each made up of many small molecules called monomers. There are natural polymers like cellulose and amber. There are man-made polymers like nylons, plastic, and PVC.

DO: Playing with Science

Review Game: Periodic Table Match-up

Materials
- ☒ Periodic Table Match-up from Elemental Science

Procedure
1. Download the game templates from the following website:
   - https://elementalscience.com/collections/free-printable-games/products/chemistry-game-periodic-table-match-up-free-ebook
2. Play Periodic Table Match-up according to the directions included in the game packet.

(Optional) STEAM Projects

Multi-chapter Activities
- **PERIODIC TABLE PROJECT** – This chapter, there is nothing to add to the periodic table. Instead, spend the time reviewing what you have done so far.

Activities For This Chapter
- **BIOPLASTIC** – Have the students make a bioplastic out of vegetable oil, cornstarch, water, food coloring, a plastic bag, and an eyedropper. In the bag, mix 3 tablespoons of cornstarch, 3 tablespoons of water, 8 to 10 drops of vegetable oil, and a few drops of food coloring. Have the students mix the ingredients thoroughly. Then, seal the bag halfway, place it on a plate, and place the bag in the microwave on high for 25 to 30 seconds. (The mixture should bubble a bit and become somewhat transparent.) Use a hot mitt to remove the baggie, and let it cool for a bit. Once it is cool enough to handle, you can shape the plastic into what the students desire. Then, let it sit overnight to completely harden.

- **POLYMER SLIME** – Have the students make their own polymer slime. You will need white (or clear gel) glue, water, a plastic baggie, and some Borax (the laundry booster, not the laundry detergent). Begin by mixing 4 oz of glue with 4 oz of water in a plastic bag. Next, in a separate cup, mix a quarter cup of water with half a teaspoon of Borax. Add the Borax solution to the baggie, and massage the bag for a few minutes until a nice, firm slime has formed. Then, pull the slime out of the baggie, and let the students have fun with their polymer.

APPENDIX

Lab Report Sheet

Title

_____

Hypothesis (What I Think Will Happen)

_____

_____

_____

_____

Materials (What We Used)

_____   _____

_____   _____

_____   _____

Procedure (What We Did)

_____

_____

_____

_____

_____

_____

_____

_____

_____
_____
_____
_____

Observations and Results (What I Saw and Measured)

_____
_____
_____
_____
_____
_____
_____
_____
_____
_____

Conclusion (What I Learned)

_____
_____
_____
_____
_____
_____

Transition Metal Hunt

21 **Sc** Scandium 44.96	22 **Ti** Titanium 47.87	23 **V** Vanadium 50.94	24 **Cr** Chromium 52.00	25 **Mn** Manganese 54.94	26 **Fe** Iron 55.85	27 **Co** Cobalt 58.93	28 **Ni** Nickel 58.69	29 **Cu** Copper 63.55	30 **Zn** Zinc 65.39
39 **Y** Yttrium 88.91	40 **Zr** Zirconium 91.22	41 **Nb** Niobium 92.91	42 **Mo** Molybdenum 95.94	43 **Tc** Technetium 98.91	44 **Ru** Ruthenium 101.1	45 **Rh** Rhodium 102.9	46 **Pd** Palladium 106.4	47 **Ag** Silver 107.9	48 **Cd** Cadmium 112.4
*71 **Lu** Lutetium 175.0	72 **Hf** Hafnium 178.5	73 **Ta** Tantalum 181.0	74 **W** Tungsten 183.9	75 **Re** Rhenium 186.2	76 **Os** Osmium 190.2	77 **Ir** Iridium 192.2	78 **Pt** Platinum 195.1	79 **Au** Gold 197.0	80 **Hg** Mercury 200.6

Many of the transition metals can be found in your house! Today, you are going to hunt around your home looking for some of the elements above. You can look anywhere you have permission to do so. (Be sure to check the labels in your pantry and medicine cabinet as well!) Here are a few ideas of items you can look for:

- ☑ Jewelry, which is often made from gold, silver, or platinum.
- ☑ Coins, which contain copper and nickel.
- ☑ Stainless steel, which is combination of iron, vanadium, nickel, tungsten, and more.
- ☑ Magnets are usually made from iron.
- ☑ Antiperspirant contains zirconium.
- ☑ Light bulb filaments are made from tungsten.
- ☑ Bicycle frames are sometimes made of titanium.
- ☑ Anything with Vitamin B12, which contains cobalt.
- ☑ Fishing lures, which often contain lead.
- ☑ Hand tools are often coated with chrom-moly steel, which contains chromium and molybdenum.
- ☑ Diaper cream often contains zinc.
- ☑ Rechargeable batteries can contain both nickel and cadmium.

1																	2
H Hydrogen 1.008																	**He** Helium 4.003
3 **Li** Lithium 6.941	4 **Be** Beryllium 9.012											5 **B** Boron 10.81	6 **C** Carbon 12.01	7 **N** Nitrogen 14.01	8 **O** Oxygen 16.00	9 **F** Fluorine 19.00	10 **Ne** Neon 20.18
11 **Na** Sodium 22.99	12 **Mg** Magnesium 24.31											13 **Al** Aluminum 26.98	14 **Si** Silicon 28.09	15 **P** Phosphorus 30.97	16 **S** Sulfur 32.07	17 **Cl** Chlorine 35.45	18 **Ar** Argon 39.95
19 **K** Potassium 39.10	20 **Ca** Calcium 40.08	21 **Sc** Scandium 44.96	22 **Ti** Titanium 47.87	23 **V** Vanadium 50.94	24 **Cr** Chromium 52.00	25 **Mn** Manganese 54.94	26 **Fe** Iron 55.85	27 **Co** Cobalt 58.93	28 **Ni** Nickel 58.69	29 **Cu** Copper 63.55	30 **Zn** Zinc 65.39	31 **Ga** Gallium 69.72	32 **Ge** Germanium 72.61	33 **As** Arsenic 74.92	34 **Se** Selenium 78.96	35 **Br** Bromine 79.90	36 **Kr** Krypton 83.80
37 **Rb** Rubidium 85.47	38 **Sr** Strontium 87.62	39 **Y** Yttrium 88.91	40 **Zr** Zirconium 91.22	41 **Nb** Niobium 92.91	42 **Mo** Molybdenum 95.94	43 **Tc** Technetium 98.91	44 **Ru** Ruthenium 101.1	45 **Rh** Rhodium 102.9	46 **Pd** Palladium 106.4	47 **Ag** Silver 107.9	48 **Cd** Cadmium 112.4	49 **In** Indium 114.8	50 **Sn** Tin 118.7	51 **Sb** Antimony 121.8	52 **Te** Tellurium 127.6	53 **I** Iodine 126.9	54 **Xe** Xenon 131.3
55 **Cs** Cesium 132.9	56 **Ba** Barium 137.3	*71 **Lu** Lutetium 175.0	72 **Hf** Hafnium 178.5	73 **Ta** Tantalum 181.0	74 **W** Tungsten 183.9	75 **Re** Rhenium 186.2	76 **Os** Osmium 190.2	77 **Ir** Iridium 192.2	78 **Pt** Platinum 195.1	79 **Au** Gold 197.0	80 **Hg** Mercury 200.6	81 **Tl** Thallium 204.4	82 **Pb** Lead 207.2	83 **Bi** Bismuth 209.0	84 **Po** Polonium [209]	85 **At** Astatine [210]	86 **Rn** Radon [222]
87 **Fr** Francium [223]	88 **Ra** Radium [226]	**103 **Lr** Lawrencium [262]	104 **Rf** Rutherfordium [261]	105 **Db** Dubnium [262]	106 **Sg** Seaborgium [266]	107 **Bh** Bohrium [264]	108 **Hs** Hassium [269]	109 **Mt** Meitnerium [268]	110 **Ds** Darmstadtium [272]	111 **Rg** Roentgenium [272]	112 **Cn** Copernicium [285]	113 **Nh** Nihonium [286]	114 **Fl** Flerovium [289]	115 **Mc** Moscovium [289]	116 **Lv** Livermorium [293]	117 **Ts** Tennessine [294]	118 **Og** Oganesson [294]

*Lanthanides

57 **La** Lanthanum 138.9	58 **Ce** Cerium 140.1	59 **Pr** Praseodymium 140.9	60 **Nd** Neodymium 144.2	61 **Pm** Promethium [145]	62 **Sm** Samarium 150.4	63 **Eu** Europium 152.0	64 **Gd** Gadolinium 157.3	65 **Tb** Terbium 158.9	66 **Dy** Dysprosium 162.5	67 **Ho** Holmium 164.9	68 **Er** Erbium 167.3	69 **Tm** Thulium 168.9	70 **Yb** Ytterbium 173.0

**Actinides

89 **Ac** Actinium [227]	90 **Th** Thorium 232.0	91 **Pa** Protactinium 231.0	92 **U** Uranium 238.0	93 **Np** Neptunium [237]	94 **Pu** Plutonium [244]	95 **Am** Americium [243]	96 **Cm** Curium [247]	97 **Bk** Berkelium [247]	98 **Cf** Californium [251]	99 **Es** Einsteinium [252]	100 **Fm** Fermium [257]	101 **Md** Mendelevium [258]	102 **No** Nobelium [259]

GLOSSARY

Chemistry Glossary

A

- AIR – A mixture of gases that form a protective layer around the Earth.
- ALLOY – A mixture of two or more metals or a metal and a nonmetal.
- ATOM – The tiny building blocks that make up everything in the universe.
- ATOMIC MASS – The average mass number of the atoms in a sample of an element.
- ATOMIC NUMBER – The number of protons in the nucleus of an atom.

B

C

- CHEMICAL BOND – A force that holds together two or more atoms.
- CHEMICAL REACTION – An occurrence where the atoms in substances are rearranged to form new substances.
- CHEMICAL SYMBOL – A shorthand way of representing a specific element in formulae and equations.

D

E

- ELEMENT – A substance made up of one type of atom, which cannot be broken down by chemical reaction to form a simpler substance.
- ESSENTIAL ELEMENT – An element that is essential to life on Earth, such as carbon, hydrogen, nitrogen, or oxygen.

F

G

H

I

- INERT – An element that is completely nonreactive.
- ION – An atom or group of atoms that has become charged by gaining or losing one or more electrons.
- ISOTOPE – An atom that has a different number of neutrons and so has a different mass number from the other atoms of an element.

J

K

L

M

- MAGNET – An object that attracts iron, steel, and metals.
- METAL – The largest class of elements, usually shiny and solid at room temperature.
- METALLOID – An element that shares some of the properties of metals and nonmetals.
- MIXTURE – A combination of two or more elements that are not chemically bonded together.
- MOLECULE – A substance made up of two or more atoms that are chemically bonded.

N

- NONMETAL – A class of elements that can be non-shiny solids or gases.

O

P

- POOR METAL – A group of metals that are soft and weak.

Q

R

- RADIOACTIVE DECAY – The process by which a nucleus ejects particles through radiation becoming the nucleus of a series of different elements until stability is reached.
- REACTIVE – The tendency of a substance to react with other substances.
- REDOX REACTION – A chemical reaction that involves the transfer of electrons.

S

- SEMICONDUCTOR – A type of material that acts as a conductor or as an insulator depending on its temperature.
- SOLUTION – A mixture that consists of a substance dissolved in a liquid.
- STATES OF MATTER – The different forms in which a substance can exist: solid, liquid, and gas.

T

U

V

W

X

Y

Z

BOOK LIST

Additional Library Books Listed By Chapter

Chapter 1

- *Atoms and Molecules (Why Chemistry Matters)* by Molly Aloian
- *Atoms and Molecules (My Science Library)* by Tracy Nelson Maurer

Chapter 2

- *What Are Atoms? (Rookie Read-About Science)* by Lisa Trumbauer
- *Atoms and Molecules (Building Blocks of Matter)* by Richard and Louise Spilsbury
- *Atoms (Simply Science)* by Melissa Stewart

Chapter 3

- *The Mystery of the Periodic Table (Living History Library)* by Benjamin D. Wiker, Jeanne Bendick and Theodore Schluenderfritz
- *The Periodic Table (True Books: Elements)* by Salvatore Tocci
- *Hydrogen and the Noble Gases (True Books: Elements)* by Salvatore Tocci
- *Hydrogen: Running on Water (Energy Revolution)* by Niki Walker

Chapter 4

- *The Alkali Metals: Lithium, Sodium, Potassium, Rubidium, Cesium, Francium (Understanding the Elements of the Periodic Table)* by Kristi Lew
- *Sodium (Elements)* by Anne O'Daly
- *Sodium (True Books: Elements)* by Salvatore Tocci
- *Potassium (Elements)* by Chris Woodford
- *Mix It Up! Solution or Mixture?* by Tracy Nelson Maurer

Chapter 5

- *The Alkaline Earth Metals: Beryllium, Magnesium, Calcium, Strontium, Barium, Radium (Understanding the Elements of the Periodic Table)* by Bridget Heos
- *Calcium (True Books: Elements)* by Salvatore Tocci
- *Magnesium (The Elements)* by Colin Uttley
- *Mixtures and Solutions (Building Blocks of Matter)* by Richard Spilsbury and Louise Spilsbury

Chapter 6

- *The Transition Elements: The 37 Transition Metals (Understanding the Elements of the Periodic Table)* by Mary-Lane Kamberg
- *Gold (The Elements)* by Sarah Angliss
- *Gold (True Books)* by Salvatore Tocci
- *What Is the World Made Of? All About Solids, Liquids, and Gases (Let's-Read-and-Find Out Science)* by Kathleen Weidner Zoehfeld and Paul Meisel
- *Solids, Liquids, And Gases (Rookie Read-About Science)* by Ginger Garrett

Chapter 7

- *Zinc (True Books)* by Salvatore Tocci
- *Zinc (Elements)* by Leon Gray
- *Iron (Elements)* by Giles Sparrow
- *From Iron to Car (Start to Finish, Second Series)* by Shannon Zemlicka
- *The Story of Iron (First Book)* by Karen Fitzgerald

Chapter 8

- *The Lanthanides (Elements) by Richard Beatty*
- *What Makes a Magnet? (Let's-Read-and-Find-Out Science 2)* by Franklyn M. Branley and True Kelley
- *What Magnets Can Do (Rookie Read-About Science)* by Allan Fowler

Chapter 9

- *Radioactive Elements* by Tom Jackson
- *The 15 Lanthanides and the 15 Actinides (Understanding the Elements of the Periodic Table)* by Kristi Lew
- *Nuclear Energy: Amazing Atoms (Powering Our World)* by Amy S. Hansen
- *Nuclear Energy (Discovery Channel School Science)* by Michael Burgan and Nancy Cohen

Chapter 10

- *The Boron Elements: Boron, Aluminum, Gallium, Indium, Thallium (Understanding the Elements of the Periodic Table)* by Heather Hasan
- *Aluminum* by Heather Hasan
- *Lead (Understanding the Elements of the Periodic Table)* by Kristi Lew

Chapter 11

- *The Carbon Elements: Carbon, Silicon, Germanium, Tin, Lead (Understanding the Elements of the Periodic Table)* by Brian Belval
- *The Invention of the Silicon Chip: A Revolution in Daily Life* by Windsor Chorlton

Chapter 12

- *Nonmetals (Material Matters/Freestyle Express)* by Carol Baldwin
- *Carbon* by Linda Saucerman
- *Carbon (True Books: Elements)* by Salvatore Tocci
- *Phosphorus (Elements)* by Richard Beatty
- *Sulfur (The Elements)* by Richard Beatty

Chapter 13

- *The Nitrogen Elements (Understanding the Elements of the Periodic Table)* by Greg Roza
- *The Oxygen Elements: Oxygen, Sulfur, Selenium, Tellurium, Polonium (Understanding the Elements of the Periodic Table)* by Laura La Bella
- *Nitrogen (True Books: Elements)* by Salvatore Tocci
- *Oxygen (True Books: Elements)* by Salvatore Tocci

Chapter 14

- *Learn about Halogens with Bearific® (Bearific® Learning Series)* by Katelyn Lonas
- *Fluorine (Understanding the Elements of the Periodic Table)* by Heather Hasan

CHAPTER 15

- *Chlorine (True Books)* by Salvatore Tocci
- *The Elements: Iodine* by Leon Gray
- *Iodine (Understanding the Elements of the Periodic Table)* by Kristi Lew

CHAPTER 16

- *Hydrogen and the Noble Gases (True Books: Elements)* by Salvatore Tocci
- *Hooray for Helium!: Understanding the 2nd Most Common Element (The Chem Kids)* by Blake Washington and Mallette Pagano

CHAPTER 17

- *Air Is All Around You (Let's-Read-and-Find... Science 1)* by Franklyn M. Branley
- *Air: Outside, Inside, and All Around (Amazing Science)* by Darlene R. Stille

CHAPTER 18

- *Plastic (Everyday Materials)* by Andrew Langley
- *Plastic, Ahoy!: Investigating the Great Pacific Garbage Patch* by Patricia Newman and Annie Crawley
- *The Adventures of a Plastic Bottle: A Story About Recycling (Little Green Books)* by Alison Inches and Pete Whitehead
- *From Plastic to Soccer Ball (Start to Finish: Sports Gear)* by Robin Nelson

QUIZZES

Chemistry Quiz #1
Chapters 2 and 3

1. Match the terms.

   ____ Atom

   ____ Atomic Number

   ____ Atomic Mass

   ____ Chemical Symbol

   ____ Element

   ____ Isotope

   A. The tiny building blocks that make up everything in the universe.

   B. A substance made up of one type of atom, which cannot be broken down by chemical reaction to form a simpler substance.

   C. An atom that has a different number of neutrons and so has a different mass number from the other atoms of an element.

   D. The number of protons in the nucleus of an atom.

   E. The average mass number of the atoms in a sample of an element.

   F. A shorthand way of representing a specific element in formulae and equations.

2. Match the following subatomic particles with their charge.

   Proton   Neutral

   Electron   Negative

   Neutron   Positive

The Sassafras Guide to Chemistry ~ Quizzes

3. **True or False:** An isotope is an atom that has a different number of neutrons.

4. **True or False:** The periodic table was first designed by Dmitri Mendeleev.

5. **True or False:** An element is made up of multiple different atoms.

6. Hydrogen exists as a _____ on Earth.

7. Weak bases taste (sour / bitter). Weak acids taste (sour / bitter).

Chemistry Quiz #2
Chapters 4 and 5

1. Match the terms.

   ____ Mixture

   ____ Reactive

   ____ Solution

   A. A mixture that consists of a substance dissolved in a liquid.

   B. A combination of two or more elements that are not chemically bonded together.

   C. The tendency of a substance to react with other substances.

2. **True or False:** The alkali metals are a very reactive group.

3. _____ reacts quickly with chlorine to form table salt.

4. **True or False:** Humans can make potassium, so we don't need to get it through our diet.

5. What are two characteristics of alkaline earth metals?

_____

_____

6. **True or False:** Magnesium is a gas that burns with a bright purple-blue light.

7. Name two places where you can find calcium-containing compounds.

_____

_____

8. The substances in a mixture (are / are not) chemically bonded.

Chemistry Quiz #3
Chapters 6 and 7

1. Match the terms.

    ____ Alloy

    ____ Metal

    ____ Redox Reaction

    ____ States of Matter

    A. The different forms in which a substance can exist: solid, liquid, and gas.

    B. The largest class of elements, usually they are shiny and solid at room temperature.

    C. A chemical reaction that involves the transfer of electrons.

    D. A mixture of two or more metals or a metal and a nonmetal.

2. What are the three states of matter on Earth?

    _____

    _____

21 **Sc** Scandium 44.96	22 **Ti** Titanium 47.87	23 **V** Vanadium 50.94	24 **Cr** Chromium 52.00	25 **Mn** Manganese 54.94	26 **Fe** Iron 55.85	27 **Co** Cobalt 58.93	28 **Ni** Nickel 58.69	29 **Cu** Copper 63.55	30 **Zn** Zinc 65.39
39 **Y** Yttrium 88.91	40 **Zr** Zirconium 91.22	41 **Nb** Niobium 92.91	42 **Mo** Molybdenum 95.94	43 **Tc** Technetium 98.91	44 **Ru** Ruthenium 101.1	45 **Rh** Rhodium 102.9	46 **Pd** Palladium 106.4	47 **Ag** Silver 107.9	48 **Cd** Cadmium 112.4
* 71 **Lu** Lutetium 175.0	72 **Hf** Hafnium 178.5	73 **Ta** Tantalum 181.0	74 **W** Tungsten 183.9	75 **Re** Rhenium 186.2	76 **Os** Osmium 190.2	77 **Ir** Iridium 192.2	78 **Pt** Platinum 195.1	79 **Au** Gold 197.0	80 **Hg** Mercury 200.6

The Sassafras Guide to Chemistry ~ Quizzes

3. The amazing ability of transition metals is that they can _____ with a variety of other elements to form alloys.

4. **True or False:** Gold is rarely found in its pure form in nature.

5. What transition metal is often used to coat metals to protect them from oxidation?
_____

6. **True or False:** Iron can be found in the core of the Earth.

7. Oxidation and reduction reactions involve the movement of _____ in molecules and atoms.

Chemistry Quiz #4
Chapters 8 and 9

1. Match the terms.

   ____ Magnet

   ____ Radioactive Decay

   A. The process by which a nucleus ejects particles through radiation, becoming the nucleus of a series of different elements until stability is reached.

   B. An object that attracts iron, steel, and metals.

2. **True or False:** For magnets, like poles attract each other, whereas unlike poles repel.

3. **True or False:** Many of the elements in lanthanide group are naturally occurring.

4. Neodymium is (not / very) magnetic.

57	58	59	60	61	62	63	64	65	66	67	68	69	70
La	**Ce**	**Pr**	**Nd**	**Pm**	**Sm**	**Eu**	**Gd**	**Tb**	**Dy**	**Ho**	**Er**	**Tm**	**Yb**
Lanthanum	Cerium	Praseodymium	Neodymium	Promethium	Samarium	Europium	Gadolinium	Terbium	Dysprosium	Holmium	Erbium	Thulium	Ytterbium
138.9	140.1	140.9	144.2	[145]	150.4	152.0	157.3	158.9	162.5	164.9	167.3	168.9	173.0
89	90	91	92	93	94	95	96	97	98	99	100	101	102
Ac	**Th**	**Pa**	**U**	**Np**	**Pu**	**Am**	**Cm**	**Bk**	**Cf**	**Es**	**Fm**	**Md**	**No**
Actinium	Thorium	Protactinium	Uranium	Neptunium	Plutonium	Americium	Curium	Berkelium	Californium	Einsteinium	Fermium	Mendelevium	Nobelium
[227]	232.0	231.0	238.0	[237]	[244]	[243]	[247]	[247]	[251]	[252]	[257]	[258]	[259]

5. **True or False:** Many of the elements in the actinide group are not radioactive.

6. Uranium is often used in _____.

        generating power   purifying water   cleaning up spills

7. Fill in the blanks with alpha, beta, and gamma.

    _____ particles consist of two protons and two neutrons.

    _____ particles are high-energy electromagnetic waves.

    _____ particles are extremely high-energy electrons.

Chemistry Quiz #5
Chapters 10 and 11

1. Match the terms.

   ____ Metalloid

   ____ Poor metal

   ____ Semiconductor

   A. A type of material that acts as a conductor or as an insulator depending on its temperature.

   B. A group of metals that are soft and weak.

   C. An element that shares some of the properties of metals and nonmetals.

2. The periodic table shows _____ between the elements.

3. What are two characteristics of main group metals?

   _____

   _____

   _____

4. **True or False:** Silicone is a common component in electronics.

The Sassafras Guide to Chemistry ~ Quizzes

151

5. What are two characteristics of metalloids?

   _____

   _____

6. Aluminum is (a rare / an abundant) element on Earth.

7. _____ is the ability of a material to conduct, or pass along, electricity or heat.

Chemistry Quiz #6
Chapters 12 and 13

1. Match the terms.

    ____ Essential Element

    ____ Nonmetal

    A. An element that is essential to life on Earth, such as carbon, hydrogen, nitrogen, or oxygen.

    B. A class of elements that can be non-shiny solids or gases.

2. What are two characteristics of nonmetals?

    _____

    _____

3. **True or False:** Pencil lead does not contain the same element as a diamond.

4. Nitrogen makes up _____ of the air on Earth.

    20% 50% 80%

6	7	8
C	**N**	**O**
Carbon	Nitrogen	Oxygen
12.01	14.01	16.00
	15	16
	P	**S**
	Phosphorus	Sulfur
	30.97	32.07
		34
		Se
		Selenium
		78.96

The Sassafras Guide to Chemistry ~ Quizzes

5. **True or False:** Oxygen is found high up in the atmosphere as ozone.

6. What are the are six elements that are essential to all life?

   C _____

   H _____

   N _____

   O _____

   P _____

   S _____

7. Organic chemistry looks at the science behind _____ compounds.

Chemistry Quiz #7
Chapters 14 and 15

1. Match the terms.

   ____ Chemical Bond

   ____ Ion

   A. An atom or group of atoms that has become charged by gaining or losing one or more electrons.

   B. A force that holds together two or more atoms.

2. **True or False:** Minerals can be deposited in the desert through evaporation.

3. **True or False:** The elements in the halogens group are not very reactive.

4. _____ is a halogen found in table salt.

5. **True or False:** Iodine is added to table salt.

9
F
Fluorine
19.00

17
Cl
Chlorine
35.45

35
Br
Bromine
79.90

53
I
Iodine
126.9

85
At
Astatine
[210]

117
Ts
Tennessine
[294]

6. _____ is method of separating compounds by passing an electrical current through a solution with the compound.

7. Fill in the blanks with covalent, ionic, and metallic.

In _____ bonding an electron is gained or lost.

In _____ bonding electrons are free to travel within a lattice.

In _____ bonding an electron is shared between two atoms.

Chemistry Quiz #8
Chapters 16 and 17

1. Match the terms.

   ____ Air   A. An element that is completely nonreactive.

                     B. A mixture of gases that form a protective layer around the Earth.

   ____ Inert

2. The noble gases are the (most / least) reactive elements in the periodic table.

3. **True or False:** Helium is heavier than air.

4. When neon comes in contact with electrical energy, it is _____.

   sluggish   excited   unchanged

2
He
Helium
4.003

10
Ne
Neon
20.18

18
Ar
Argon
39.95

36
Kr
Krypton
83.80

54
Xe
Xenon
131.3

86
Rn
Radon
[222]

118
Og
Oganesson
[294]

5. Circle the two main gases that are found in air.

    oxygen   argon   nitrogen   chlorine

6. Distillation is a method of separating two or more _____.

    solids   liquids   gases

Made in United States
North Haven, CT
05 June 2023